Mountain Biking in the Adirondacks

Introduction

This guide for mountain bike riding in the Adirondack Park (park) describes rides over a range of difficulty. A couple are on roads where cars might be seen, but the rest are trails through the woods, some easy and some that climb and descend, filled with rocks, roots and sometimes mud. They are scenic, fun, and often exciting and challenging. The trails go through public land except for a few forays into privately owned sections where public use is allowed. The 25 rides in the guide are numbered, chapters 1 through 25. They are each rated according to their skill level: beginner, intermediate or expert. Pick a ride near your skill level and you will find some great riding!

Mountain Biking in the Adirondacks: 25 Trail Riding Adventures

Gary Thomann

Singletrack Publishing
Scotia, New York

Note to the reader

Trail conditions for rides in this guidebook are described as they were at the time I rode them. Trail conditions change, sometimes rapidly, according to weather and trail maintenance. Bridges wash out or are replaced, a storm blows down trees across the trail, a beaver dam floods the trail, a maintenance crew works on the trail, etc. In each description I have tried to indicate the general condition of the trail. As a trail user, you should expect to find some difference between what I describe and what you actually experience on your rides. If you find significant changes I would appreciate a note from you about them. The publishing mailing address is below.

Cover design and book design by Spear Design™
Front cover photo by Nancie Battaglia
Back cover photo provided by Art Today
Maps by Gary C. Thomann, ©2001
Interior photos by: Gary C. Thomann
                             Richard Gibbs
                             Darryl Caron
                             Carie MacDonald

Published by: Singletrack Publishing
                             222 S Ten Broeck St, Apt 7
                             Scotia NY 12302

ISBN: 0-9710937-0-9

Acknowledgements

I had a lot of help getting this book written, reviewed and published. Paul Capone originally helped me pick out a number of rides for the guide. Many riders helped explore the trails, participated in arguments about where we were, and assisted in finding the way back to the trailhead. I would particularly like to thank Dick Gibbs, Joe Dalton, Tim Moran, Ben Hill and Sam Armao for riding with me. Darryl Caron, editor of "Adirondack Sports & Fitness" got me started again after I had given up on the guide, and also helped publish it. Dick, Darryl, Paul, Sharon Gibbs, Robin Butkus and Kristina Flanders reviewed and edited the guide and their work is greatly appreciated; editing is much more difficult and a lot less fun than riding. The excellent book design is by Carie MacDonald of Spear Design™. Finally, thanks to Nancie Battaglia for the sweet cover photo. The debts I owe these people will of course be repaid by taking them on mountain bike rides!

Table of Contents

SECTION 4 - Southwest

SECTION 5 - Northwest

SECTION 6 - Additional Resources

Getting Started

What You Need besides this Guide

You just stepped off the airplane, want to go riding, and somehow found a copy of this book. What else do you need? Well, first of course you need a bike and helmet. If you didn't bring yours, go to a local bike store and buy or rent them. There is a list of bicycle stores in the Additional Resources section at the end of this guide. Bike stores are also a good place to get up to date information on local trails and trail conditions. Second, you need an ordinary road map. The Adirondack Park is 120 miles across, and the rides are widely scattered. Buy one at a convenience store; they are so numerous that I have not tried to list their locations. Just stop at the first one you see. Third, you need a compass. Buy one at a local outdoor store, or from one listed at the end of this guide. Finally, you need a computer (odometer) on your bike, or on one of the bikes in the group you are riding in. This can be purchased at one of the bike stores. There is additional discussion of bike computers in the Bike and Other Equipment section. I consider the road map, compass and odometer as required equipment. There is additional equipment discussed below that is helpful, but not required.

Each ride listed here has a map which covers the trail you will be riding. You may wish to have a set of hiking maps that show larger areas than each individual map in this small format book. There are two well known hiking map sets for the park, listed in the Additional Resources section. The maps can be purchased at outdoor stores, and at some bookstores. There is also a list of bookstores at the end of the guide.

You will learn in the next section that Adirondack Park mountain bike trail riding is allowed only in certain areas of public land, zoned (classified) "Wild Forest." Included in the guide is an illustration that outlines these wild forest areas, but it cannot show the area boundaries in great detail. There are several large maps which do show the park land classifications in considerable detail, and they aid in understanding use of the park. These maps are listed in the Additional Resources section along with instructions for obtaining them.

Each ride map in this guide has a Global Positioning System (GPS) grid overlay, and you can use a small GPS unit to track your position. Although it doesn't replace common sense, GPS can help you navigate. If you are nervous about getting lost, or intend to do a lot of exploring, consider buying one. A list of local Adirondack stores that sell GPS equipment is included in the

Additional Resources section. If you dive into GPS literature you may read about differential GPS (DGPS), DPGS ready, ground reference stations, etc. Don't worry about this, you need only a simple unit available for $100 to $150 that can take readings, store a few of them, and display heading and distance back to previously stored locations. You should also read the additional discussion on GPS limitations in the Map Description section later in the guide.

If you want even more information about where you are, an altimeter will monitor your elevation. A barometric altimeter is best for doing this; purchase one at an outdoor store. Although they are interesting to use, an altimeter is not necessary.

I recommend you read the information about bike set-up in the Bike and Other Equipment section. It will help select a rental bike if you need one, or may convince you to change something on the bike you already have. After reading the section, head for one of the listed bike stores if you need equipment.

As you tour the park and enjoy the recreation and scenic beauty in it, you will want to learn more about it. There are hundreds, if not thousands, of books and pamphlets on the park, available at book stores listed in the Additional Resources section.

I suggest you read the rest of the explanatory material in this guide, but if you have to go riding right now, here are the 25 rides grouped by level of difficulty. For a first ride, pick one you have the skills for.

Ride Ratings

Beginner rides

The following are beginner rides—All you need is a bike, helmet and the ride description.

- Mitchell Ponds and Beaver Lake (ch. 18)
- Old Road to Santanoni Preserve (ch. 11)
- Hays Brook Truck Trail (ch. 12)
- Stony Pond (ch. 1)
- Harrisburg Lake to Bakertown Bridge (ch. 2)
- Perkins Clearing (ch. 19)

Intermediate rides

Next are the intermediate rides–lots of fun on a mountain bike if you have some bike handling skills and fitness. You should have the skill to ride through rock gardens full of head size rocks, handle roots and logs up to six inches in diameter, on both level ground and descents.

- Floodwood Loop (ch. 13)
- Pumpkin Hollow to the Pine Orchard (ch. 3)
- Sargent Ponds to Raquette Lake (ch. 20)
- Burntbridge Pond Trail (ch. 24)
- Deer Pond Loop (ch. 14)
- Meacham Lake to Debar Meadow (ch. 15)
- Cranberry Lake Loop (ch. 25)
- Pine Pond (ch. 16)
- Pumpkin Hollow to Wilcox Lake (ch. 4)
- Moose Mountain Pond & Bass Lake (ch. 17)
- McKeever - Bear Creek Loop (ch. 21)
- Beech Mountain/Blackberry Alley (ch. 5)
- Brownell Camp to Bakertown Bridge (ch. 6)

Expert rides

Finally there are the expert rated rides–exciting but challenging. You will find big rocks, corduroy and sometimes steep climbs and descents on these adventures.

- Irving Pond - Peters Corners Loop (ch. 22)
- Lake George Northwest Bay Trail (ch. 7)
- Stewart Landing - Caroga Lake Loop (ch. 23)
- Pumpkin Hollow to Creek Road (ch. 8)
- Irishtown-Minerva Stream Trail (ch. 9)
- Knapp Estate Hogtown Loop (ch. 10)

The Park

The Adirondack Park in northern New York (NY) is a mecca of scenery, recreation and history, containing forests, mountains, lakes, rivers, marshes, farmland, roads and small towns on about 6 million acres of private and public land. The actual distribution at the end of 1996 was 3,053,858 acres of privately owned land, 2,432,729 acres of publicly owned land, and 334,608 acres of water. Since that time, additional public land has been added. The following map shows the park boundaries (familiarly called the "blue line"), the counties, and some of the roads and towns/villages within the park.

The permanent park population is about 130,000 in its 105 towns and villages, with an additional 200,000 seasonal. Fourteen percent of the park is classified as wetland; there are 1,200 mi of designated river corridors, and over 2,000 mi of trails. The Adirondack Council, a local non-profit organization,

Adirondack Park boundaries

lists boreal forest, lake, upland forest, hardwood forest, brook, river, bog, beaver flow, marsh, farm fields, river valley and alpine meadow as wildlife habitat areas in the park. The highest point in the park is the peak of Mount Marcy at 5344 ft (1630 m); the lowest elevation is a few hundred feet. The bedrock of much of the park is an ancient geological formation, estimated to be 1.2 billion years old.

A partial list of summer recreation in the park is hiking, canoeing, kayaking, caving, rock climbing, fishing, bird watching, camping, horseback riding and mountain biking. In the winter there is downhill skiing, XC skiing, snowshoeing, ice climbing, ice fishing, dog sledding, snowmobile riding, etc. Let's look a little closer at the park, from a mountain biking point of view.

Park Regulations

The park has a rather complicated regulatory structure, which an aspiring mountain bike rider needs to understand, since it is this regulatory framework that largely determines where off road riding is allowed. First, the park has its own zoning authority, the Adirondack Park Agency (APA), located in Ray Brook. The address, phone number and web site for the APA are listed in the Additional Resources section at the end of this guide. Similar information is supplied there for other agencies mentioned in this book.

The APA has divided the park land into about 15 different classifications, all of which fortunately you don't need to learn. First, the details of the privately owned land classifications can be disregarded for our use. The remaining public land in the Adirondack Park is called Forest Preserve, divided into seven APA classifications, but only four are important for most recreational users, including mountain bikers. These four classifications are: Wilderness, Canoe Area, Primitive and Wild Forest (WF). At the end of 1996, according to the APA there were 1,034,106 acres of Wilderness, 50,848 of Primitive, 17,013 of Canoe Area and 1,275,559 of Wild Forest.

The classification largely determines the allowed recreational use. Hiking, skiing, canoeing, rock climbing and similar pursuits are allowed in any of the four areas. Snowmobiles are allowed only in the WF designated areas. All Terrain Vehicles (ATV's), dirt bikes and similar motorized equipment are banned in all, or almost all areas. At the time of publication (2001), mountain bike riding is not allowed in Wilderness lands. Primitive and Canoe Area zoned lands are also closed to bicycling unless a trail has been specifically designated and posted as rideable.

Fortunately, mountain bike riding is allowed on most trails in the Wild Forest classified areas, and almost all the rides described here are in WF. To group the rides in this guide, I have roughly divided the park into southeast, northeast, southwest and northwest regions. A line through the villages of Long Lake and Newcomb splits north and south, while a vertical line through Paul Smiths and Indian Lake divides east and west. The WF classified areas listed by the APA are shown in the table below. There is not an even distribution of wild forest land across the park. The northwest has the least, despite having six wild forest areas, because each of the six is small. The northwest portion of the park is dominated by privately owned forestry acreage. The largest WF areas are in the southern part of the park, and the southern part is where much of the good riding is, although it is also possible to find great rides in the northern areas. The second park illustration shows the large pieces of the WF designated land. Some small parcels are not shown. The map also shows the

Southeast	**Northeast**	**Southwest**	**Northwest**
• Lake George	• Hammond Pond	• Shaker Mountain	• Cranberry Lake
• Wilcox Lake	• Saranac Lakes	• Ferris Lake	• Whitehill
• Vanderwhacker Mountain	• Debar Mountain	• Black River	• Raquette Boreal
	• Taylor Pond	• Moose River Plains	• Horseshoe Lake
		• Independence River	• Aldrich Pond
		• Sargent Ponds	• Watson's East Triangle
		• Jessup River	
		• Fulton Chain	
		• Blue Mountain	

trailhead locations of the twenty-five rides in the guide. The rides are listed by chapter number.

There is another level of detail to the park regulation. According to NY state law, each WF area in the park will have a Unit Management Plan (UMP) and these should state in more detail what uses are allowed on each trail. The UMP's are under development in 2001. Initial examination of the draft UMP's indicates that the Wild Forest areas will remain open for riding.

The APA is the zoning agency for the Adirondack Park, but the actual

Wild Forest areas and ride locations

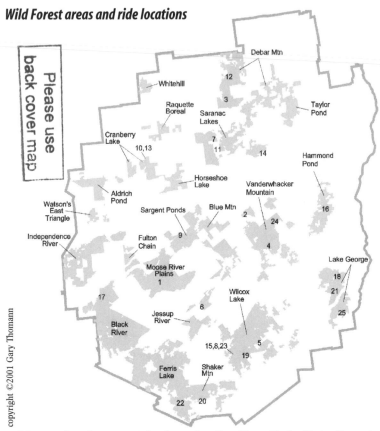

writing and enforcement is done by the New York State Department of Environmental Conservation (DEC). For example, forest rangers are DEC employees. DEC has divided the state into regions, and most of the Adirondack Park is in Regions 5 (Franklin, Clinton, Essex, Hamilton, Warren, Fulton, Saratoga and Washington counties) and 6 (Jefferson, St. Lawrence, Lewis, Oneida and Herkimer counties). Addresses and phone numbers for DEC are listed at the end of the guide. If you are unclear about the regulations in some area, call or visit the appropriate office.

Trails in the Wild Forest Areas

To a large extent, WF has a single trail system; snowmobile use in the winter and hiking in the summer. There are some exceptions to this; e.g. narrow hiking trails on which snowmobiles are not allowed. Most of this trail system is open to mountain bikes, summer and winter. Again, there are a few exceptions, such as fragile trails that DEC has closed to riding. Snowmobile trails are generally not classical singletrack trails; the machines are too big and wide to exist on very narrow trails. Instead they are 4 to 10 ft wide; they may have originally been carriage roads in existence early in U.S. history, old logging roads, or they may have been constructed specifically for hiking and snowmobile use. These trails, along with some additional singletrack hiking trails not open to snowmobiles, are what you will be riding. What are they like?

Well, these trails generally require intimate involvement. Don't expect something akin to a jeep road through the desert, where you finish the ride in about the same condition as you started, unmarred and only slightly dusty. Adirondack trails are usually damp, sometimes plain wet. There is some sandy glacial outwash soil, but much is organic. You may have to dig several feet down to find mineral soil or rock. After a ride, some of this soil (muck) is going to be stuck to you and your bike, especially if you happened to fall over while riding alongside a big muddy area. The best remedy for the bike is to just go to the car wash, clean the bike, re-oil the chain and joints on the derailleurs, and lightly oil the brake and derailleur cables. A list of local car washes is in the Additional Resources section. The best remedy for you, too, may be the car wash.

The trails are often full of loose or partly buried rocks, sized from an inch to a couple feet across. Riding these rocks is technically challenging and also great fun if you pick rides which roughly match your skill level. Where there is no soil, the trail surface will be bedrock, with occasional ledges, also a challenging and rewarding surface to ride.

The Adirondacks are heavily forested, and there are almost always roots rising above the trail surface. As big as your arm, and sometimes your leg, they snake at every angle, acute and obtuse. The roots offer another riding challenge, especially when you encounter several big roots spaced a foot or two apart.

Regular trail maintenance is required on Adirondack trails, and maintenance crews cannot keep up with the necessary work. Many of the Wild Forest trails are only lightly used, because hikers often go to the more glamorous wilderness classified areas, and the WF trails receive low maintenance priority. Occasionally there will be branches hanging out into the trail, which can scratch you. There may also be larger stuff in the trail (blowdown), over or around which you will sometimes have to carry your bike. I have not discussed trail overgrowth or blowdown in the individual ride descriptions, because they change so rapidly according to recent maintenance activities.

There are lots (I mean lots) of small streams, creeks and brooks to cross when you ride. The larger ones sometimes have a bridge across them, or a less formal structure made of shipping pallets, bailing wire, logs and old car parts. Sometimes the creek can be easily crossed on a bridge, while in other cases the structure may be one of the most challenging features of the trail. In warm weather you can ride, or try to ride, across the un-bridged streams; the crossing may be easy, or there may be a big drop from the trail surface down to the water level. The stream may have a smooth bottom, or be littered with randomly placed large rocks, not quite identifiable through the ripples on the surface. Just the stream crossings alone, whether on a bridge or through the water, will provide your riding group with discussion and amusement for months following the ride.

On some rides there are numerous trail elevation changes, with all out aerobic climbs and some so steep, long and rocky, that you will have to push your bike up them. The flip side is, of course, descents; some are smooth downward glides and others are rocky 40 percent slope challenges on which even the most experienced rider can quickly come to, or cross, that fine line between exhilaration and terror. Ascending and descending are one of the trail riding charms that you will enjoy if you select rides that match your skill level.

Wild Forest trails conform to the features of the landscape through which they run, so you never ride a straight line very long. Expect many turns, from easy swings around a wet area to sharp switchbacks. Adopt the attitude that turning is one of the most enjoyable skills of mountain bike riding and you will be fine.

Corduroy is another Adirondack trail charm, of which you may be unfamiliar. Wet boggy areas of a trail are sometimes bridged by filling them with logs laid side by side across the trail. Logs with diameters from a couple of inches to over a foot can be used. The length of corduroy surface is often just a few feet, but may be fifty feet long. Since this was a wet section of trail to begin with, as you can imagine the logs are also wet and slippery, and offer additional riding enjoyment/challenges. Most corduroy can be ridden if you make sure to hit the logs right at a ninety degree angle and get up enough speed to make it across the log section without a lot of pedaling. If you walk across

Bench cutting a section of trail.

corduroy, you still must be careful; the curved log surfaces are difficult to stand on. The presence of corduroy is usually mentioned in the ride descriptions.

Through much of the spring and summer you will share the trail with bugs, mosquitos, black flies and deer flies; you will return from your ride with at least a few bites. Wear insect repellent, keep a good attitude, keep riding at a reasonable speed and the bugs will not be anything more than a nuisance.

The trail descriptions include a difficulty rating (beginner, intermediate, expert) and the rating assumes dry conditions. That may sound like a contradiction, given what I have already said about trail wetness. However, most of the time the surfaces of the things that stick up from the trail surface

(rocks, roots and old bike parts) are dry and offer good purchase for a mountain bike tire, especially if it is inflated to a low pressure as discussed elsewhere in this guide. This is what I call dry conditions. But, if you ride in the rain, or right after a rain, expect the trail difficulty to increase one level. Rocks are slippery and roots become coated with some type of wet organic tree snot. Also be careful of the wooden bridges across streams; they can become so slippery it is even difficult to walk across them.

The finest feature of Adirondack trails is scenery, and it is everywhere. There are the classic vistas from mountain tops, big lakes, virgin growth forest and whitewater streams and the mundane, but just as beautiful ferns, small frogs, marshes and bogs. If you are observant and lucky, you can spot deer, squirrels, foxes, coyotes, beaver, otters and black bears, as well as numerous birds, including ducks, geese, ravens, wild turkey, hawks and eagles. The scenery itself is a good reason to go riding. After you ride there is often nearby swimming, or the chance to wash mud off in a rocky cold fast flowing stream. Oh, maybe I forgot to mention, you can also see various insects.

All of this may sound somewhat daunting, but it need not be. Just like downhill skiing, whitewater kayaking or rock climbing, you need to select a ride which is reasonably close to your skill level and preference, so you can be challenged but still have fun. If you attempt the Hogtown loop at Lake George, with only beginner skills you will not have fun. If you want an easy day, or are just starting to mountain bike, ride into Santanoni Preserve for scenery and adventure at the price of a few calories. As to the rocks, mud and bugs, don't be too worried; ignore this little stuff and jump right into some of the best mountain biking in the world.

The Bike and Other Equipment

Experienced riders from the local area and the Northeast know what Adirondack trail conditions will be, and know what type of mountain bike setup they like. For beginners, and riders from mud challenged areas of the country, I will attempt to provide some advice on buying or renting a bike, based on my riding experience in the Adirondacks on three different bikes.

You want a true mountain bike, long and low, with fat tires. Hybrid bikes, or what are sometimes called cross bikes, are not appropriate for Adirondack trails, although they are suitable for gravel roads and similar riding, and will work fairly well on the beginner rated rides in this guide.

You want a light bike, since you will be carrying it over logs, through streams and lifting it into your car after a long ride. Shoot for a 23 lb or lighter bike. Aluminum is a popular light frame material, and there are other exotic (read expensive) frame materials like titanium and carbon fiber. Very inexpensive bikes often have steel frames, which are heavy. Bike components (cranks, brakes, derailleurs and such) become lighter as price goes up. You don't need the most expensive racing components, but the 2nd or 3rd rated components are usually a good combination of weight and price. For example, many bikes have components made by the Shimano company. The first five Shimano categories starting from the top are XTR, Deore XT, Deore LX, Deore and

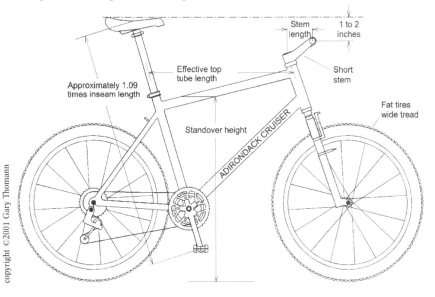

Alivio. The XTR components are light but expensive, $450 - 500 higher than the XT set. Either the XT or LX are good for a recreational bike.

Bike manufacturers specify frame sizes, but the size is not always a good guide, as the measurement method may vary from brand to brand. Some specify the distance from the center of the bottom bracket to the top of the top tube, and others the distance from center to top of the seat collar.

You should focus primarily on two other frame measurements. First, you want a bike with a low standover height (relative to your inseam length). A picture of one of my bikes is shown. From the size of the frame in comparison to the wheels, you can see I am tall. However, this bike should still be suitable for illustration. When you are standing over the frame of the bike, just in front of the saddle, you want several inches of clearance between the top tube and your crotch. On Adirondack trails there will be many instances in which you will hit rocks, roots, trees, other bikes (did I mention rocks) and the bike will come to a stop, and you will jump forward slightly to land on your feet, or take one foot out of the pedal and set it on the ground. Often you do not land on level ground. The reason for the clearance should be obvious, to both male and female riders. To provide the clearance a well designed mountain bike has a sloping top tube, and this is the frame design you want.

Many bike manufacturers list the standover heights for their frames, which is the distance from the ground to the top of the top tube at a position a few inches in front of the saddle. For bicycle purposes your inseam length is different than that when you are buying a new pair of pants. It can be measured by standing on a hard surface with socks on and feet spread a few inches. Press a book firmly into your crotch with about the pressure from a bicycle seat. The vertical distance from the floor to the top of the book is your inseam, a distance you want to be several inches greater than the frame standover height. If you are trying a bike out, just stand over the top tube and slide your hand between the top tube and your crotch; there should be a least a couple of inches of clearance.

The second important measurement is the top tube length; with a sloping top tube the measurement is the effective top tube length, as shown in the illustration. This distance should be long enough that you can fit comfortably on the bike with a short stem; 120 mm or shorter. Fitting comfortably means that with your hands grasping the handlebars, your back is at an angle of 45 degrees or so with the ground. If you have to install a longer stem to get this position, you will have too much weight over the front wheel and will be in danger of "going over the bars" when the front wheel hits a boulder or log. Don't worry about missing any bike fun. Even with a properly designed bike you will probably have plenty of opportunities for this maneuver.

Once you have a bike, you cannot change the frame measurements, so it is important to get them right. The other bike adjustments can then be made. The seat height is adjusted so your leg comes to almost full extension at the bottom of the pedal stroke. For an initial guess set the saddle to pedal distance as 1.09 times your measured inseam, as shown on the illustration bike, and then make fine adjustments from that setting. The forward/backward position of the seat is set to put your knee in proper position. Seat position should not be used to make up for deficiencies in top tube length. The "neutral" position is shown in the accompanying drawing; with the pedal cranks in horizontal position a vertical line through your kneecap bisects the pedal axis. Most riders knees are close to this alignment. Next, with the seat adjusted both in height and forward/backward, a horizontal line from the top of the saddle should pass an inch or two over the top of the handlebars. Adjustment of handlebar height can be done with spacers or using curved (riser) bars.

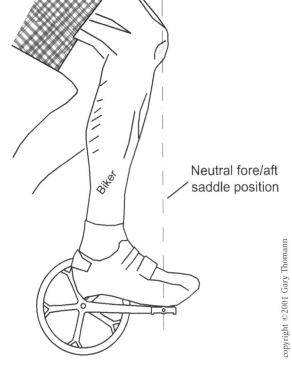

Neutral fore/aft saddle position

copyright ©2001 Gary Thomann

For Adirondack riding I like large tires (2.2" or larger) with large wide-spaced tread blocks and low tire pressures (28 - 35 lb). The large tires span cracks, hang onto the edges of rocks, and seem to work well in soft ground. The low pressures help the tire stick on slippery roots and rocks and also absorb shock. The large tread blocks throw mud well.

A front shock is highly recommended; it will help both your riding skill and comfort. You are on your own when it comes to rear suspension. With it the bike will ride smoother. However, it will also be heavier by a couple of pounds and probably require more maintenance than the single suspended (hardtail) bike, because the rear suspension adds moving parts. I like bar ends even though I don't ride with my hands on them. Use the longer bar ends that curve in quite a distance and the handlebars will slide by small trees that you invariably brush against.

In the beginning of the guide I stated the requirement for a bike computer. I feel that way because of the need to keep track of trail distance between the numerous intersections and branching trails you will encounter. A wireless unit is best. The bushes and other vegetation along a trail will snag the wires of a conventional unit, no matter how securely they are taped to the bike frame. Try to get a computer that measures to .01 mi or .01 km, because you often need to measure relative distance accurately.

I recommend the pedal/shoe systems where the cleat on the bottom of the shoe snaps into the pedal. This combination provides some security for your feet while allowing easy entrance and exit (with perhaps some practice). If you use Shimano pedals, or pedals compatible with Shimano cleats, you might wish to start with the multi-release (silver) cleats which unsnap more easily than the single release (black) cleats. I do not recommend pedals with toe straps; they are very difficult to get into on tough trails.

Carry equipment with you for making common repairs and adjustments. As you might expect, this includes a spare tube or two, a pump (or CO_2 cartridge), the hex (Allen) wrenches that fit your bike and maybe a spoke wrench. Some type of patch to repair a ripped tire can also be carried; a dollar bill or energy bar wrapper is the classic temporary fix. Carry a chain breaker. Occasionally a chain link will be bent and need to be removed. Because of all the loose sticks and branches on Adirondack trails it is fairly common to break rear derailleurs. If you ride with a group, you might have one rider carry a spare one so the broken unit can be replaced. In theory you can bypass a broken derailleur by converting your bike to single speed and then ride home in this one gear. On modern bikes that remedy rarely succeeds. The vertical rear dropouts prevent chain tightness adjustment, which is needed to make the single speed set-up work. The compass, altimeter and GPS unit have already been mentioned, and there is additional GPS discussion later.

Proper nutrition and hydration is also just common sense. Carry plenty of water or energy drink, either in water bottles or one of the backpack hydration systems. Carry your favorite food, either something healthy or Oreo's and M&M's. Carry LOTS of food. Your buddies will appreciate it.

When riding, don't wear lose fitting clothing that can snag in branches. Bicycle jerseys or windbreakers work well. On the bottom, don't wear something that significantly impairs knee movement. Classical lycra bicycle shorts or newer mountain bike shorts are good. Don't ever wear cotton, because when wet it is both heavy and cold. However, there is one use for cotton. Stick a cotton handkerchief into a ziplock bag, smash it to get all the air out, zip it tight, and put it into your pocket or pack. Halfway through the ride, when you need to clean off your glasses, it will be the only dry thing within five miles.

In warm weather wear thin synthetic socks; your feet will probably get wet and heavy socks will make for heavy feet. Of course wear a helmet. Wear full fingered gloves, your hands will bump into things. Wear glasses of some kind to protect your eyes. Use glass straps. I don't recommend sunglasses. No matter how bright the sun is, deep in the woods there is little light and many shadows, and roots and rocks sticking up into the trail are difficult to see with dark glasses. Wear

Riding with companions is not only safer, it is more enjoyable.

ones with clear lenses. Finally, carry some first aid supplies, at least a few Band-Aids and some adhesive tape.

Ride with companions, not alone. If common sense is used, mountain bike riding is safe. Still, there are things that can go wrong out in the woods, with you or the bike. I think the best riding is with a group of four or five, which provides plenty of support, company and conversation, while not being too large to keep track of everybody. If you must ride alone, do the old road into Santanoni Preserve; you probably won't have equipment problems on such an easy trail, nor are you likely to crash.

For colder weather, or winter riding, wear a windbreaker above a couple of layers of polypro or other moisture wicking material. Wear ski gloves, not mittens, so one or two fingers can hook over the brake levers. Take the pads out of your helmet and line it with a workman's hard hat liner. On the bottom wear insulated tights. There are a variety available, some that are windproof on the front. Pants over polypro are an alternative for your legs; best if the combination provides easy knee movement and the pants don't flop near the chain.

You may have problems with your feet in cold weather. Here are some suggestions, which may require the purchase of an extra inexpensive pair of bike shoes. Wear shoes that fit loosely, even with a pair of heavy socks on, so there is room for wiggling toes. Overdress the rest of your body and protect your head (the reason for the helmet liner), so blood will be sent to the extremities. Wear insulated neoprene bicycle shoe covers. Use waterproof sock covers if there will be wet areas on the trail, or streams to cross. Finally, while on the ride, dismount and walk or run a short distance every once in a while.

When to Ride

That's easy, anytime you don't have to work. Obviously, most riding is done in warm weather, but you can ride year round. Start by considering the spring when the snow cover is gone, as early as April in the southern part of the park. The spring is wet, so ride on rocky roads and trails which are not affected too much by water. I have tried to identify some of these trails in the guide. As spring continues the bugs will emerge. My advice is just keep riding and try to keep the pace fast enough to minimize the problem. Save your energy for big problems. Don't worry about small things like insects.

The summer, July, August, September is a great time to ride; you don't need much guidance there. Supposedly there will be fewer bugs in the summer, although they are still encountered. Consider recent rainfall and wetness when making trail choices. In northern areas the leaves should be changing color in September.

October and early November are great times to ride. It is (hopefully) not yet bitterly cold, the bugs are gone, and the trails are as dry as they will get. This is a good time of the year to ride the normally wet trails. Leaf color should be great in the southern areas in October.

It may sound crazy, but you can also ride in the winter. I have been riding for seven or eight

Springtime is the most likely time to see river rapids.

winters and have had many great rides. You just have to change your outlook slightly from summer riding. Dress warmly as suggested above. You don't need a lot of trails, just one or two nearby. Well traveled snowmobile trails or un-maintained town roads are great. Make the rides short, 2 hours in length; with all the clothes you have on that will be plenty of exercise. Keep track of the weather; that determines where and how you ride.

When I say keep track of the weather, I really mean try to guess what the trail surface will be. In November and December, the trail surface will harden, but there may be little or no snow on the ground. This is a great time to ride; frozen ground is an ideal surface, especially in the Adirondacks where in warmer months there is so much mud. On that 25 degree gloomy Sunday in early December take your bike and go ride a nearby trail. Do nothing special for the bike; just keep it clean and use light bicycle oil on the chain and the derailleurs; heavy oil gets too stiff in the cold.

A second winter trail condition is a foot of fresh snow. Well, you're stuck, bicycles just don't go well in deep snow. Go skiing or snowshoeing or read bike catalogs. But keep watching the weather. After a week or so, on a well used snowmobile trail, the snow will be packed hard enough to support a bike, especially if wide tires with low pressure are used (actually appropriate year round for Adirondack trails). Start riding again, same equipment and clothing as before. Traction is good or excellent. Losing all restraint and common sense, you will soon be screaming down the trail in the big ring jumping snowmobile moguls. Eventually you will land one of these jumps wrong, resulting in a huge but usually harmless snow crash. The front tire of the bike occasionally breaking through the surface or hitting an icy spot will just add to the challenge and enjoyment.

As the snowmobile trails continue to get used, they will become icy. Or, it will warm up and rain, then refreeze, resulting in icy closed roads, and no possibility of staying upright on skis. These are dream conditions for mountain biking! All you need are some studded tires; regular mountain bike tires which have sheet metal screws through them from the inside out. With these tires riding on ice is easy, down trails or across frozen lakes. Directions for obtaining or building

Studded tires provide the necessary traction on ice.

studded tires are included at the end of the guide, and some bike shops will make them for you.

Safety and Trail Etiquette

The rule for right-of-way is you don't have any. Give way to everybody, hikers, skiers, equestrians, kids, dogs and canoeists. Be especially careful around horses, they are generally not used to bikes on a trail and can shy easily. Get off your bike and let the other trail users go past. If you are riding down the trail and an oncoming hiker steps off to the side and motions you to do so, you can ride on past. User conflicts probably won't occur on a rocky tight single-track trail; you will be going so slow you couldn't surprise anybody anyway. However, you can go pretty fast descending on a wider/easier trail. When descending, watch well ahead of the bike and be prepared for surprises. ATV's and motorcycle's are not supposed to be on public trails, but you will probably meet them. When you hear them, prepare to take evasive action; they can go very fast. When riding in the winter, watch out for snowmobiles.

A second caution: do not damage the trail or the surrounding area. Be careful about skidding and dislodging trail material. On steep descents it can be almost impossible to keep the rear tire from skidding, but do your best. Do not create a new trail by riding outside the existing trail; this just results in two trails to maintain. Either ride in the existing trail or walk and carry your bike through it. During wet periods, don't ride on soft trails. Instead, ride on an old road.

Trail users are allowed to perform a certain amount of maintenance on the wild forest trails. You can throw debris off the trails, and you can clear out obstructions which are holding water on the trail. Occasionally do some maintenance work when you ride; it will help your guilt about the fast curve you skidded around. Trail users can also trim branches which overhang into the trail, but riders usually can't carry clippers/loppers for doing this. If you ride a lot, consider performing some more formal maintenance work. Various organizations, such as the Adirondack Club (ADK) sponsor trail work parties where you can learn trail skills and make new friends. It is a great privilege to have such a resource for riding; help take care of it.

The following are the six rules for mountain bikers formulated by the International Mountain Biking Association (IMBA). They are the standard rules for riding anywhere.

Ride on open trails only. *Respect trail and road closures (ask if not sure), avoid possible trespass on private land, obtain permits and authorization as may be required. Federal and State wilderness areas are closed to cycling.*

Leave no trace. *Be sensitive to the dirt beneath you. Even on open trails, you should not ride under conditions where you will leave evidence of your passing, such as on certain soils shortly after a rain. Observe the different types of soils and trail construction, practice low*

impact cycling. This also means staying on the trail and not creating any new ones. Be sure to pack out at least as much as you pack in.
Control your bicycle. *Inattention for even a second can cause problems. Obey all speed laws.*
Always yield the trail. *Make known your approach well in advance. A friendly greeting (or a bell) is considerate and works well, don't startle others. Show your respect when passing others by slowing to a walk or even stopping. Anticipate that other trail users may be around corners or in blind spots.*
Never spook animals. *All animals are startled by an unannounced approach, a sudden movement, or a loud noise. This can be dangerous for your, for others, and for the animals. Give animals extra room and time to adjust to you. In passing, use special care and follow directions of horseback riders (ask if uncertain). Running cattle and disturbing wild animals is a serious offense. Leave gates as you found them, or as marked.*
Plan Ahead. *Know your equipment, your ability, and the area in which you are riding - and prepare accordingly. Be self-sufficient at all times. Wear a helmet, keep your machine in good condition, and carry necessary supplies for changes in weather or other conditions. A well-executed trip is a satisfaction to you and not a burden or offense to others.*

Trail Descriptions and Maps

Each of the described rides in this guide has a title, five brief notes, directions to the trailhead, a fairly detailed ride description and a map. The title may be a historical name for the trail, or a name I thought matched the ride. The brief notes list total ride distance, difficulty, climbing required, time to ride and Wild Forest area.

In the brief notes at the top, the total distance you will ride is given in miles (mi) with kilometers (km) in parenthesis. Difficulty is estimated as beginner, intermediate or expert (or sometimes a combination). Any reasonably fit person can get on a mountain bike, ride on a beginner trail, and expect to have a good (and sometimes exciting) time. After a season of riding, you can attain intermediate status. Getting to be an expert rider needs more riding with other good riders, practice and maybe some lessons. The climbing required is the total required, NOT the difference in elevation between the start and finish of the ride. A 2 hr beginner ride with a couple hundred feet of climbing requires only a reasonable level of bicycle fitness. A 5 hr ride with a couple thousand feet of climbing requires considerably more fitness and probably a higher skill rating since downhill sections are often challenging. The time to do the riding is an estimate based on fairly continuous riding, but not at race speed. The WF area is the APA designated name.

The directions to the trailhead are from a reasonable start point, like an interstate exit or the center of a village. As already discussed you should have a NY state road map to help you navigate to the trailhead.

In the detailed description, distances along the trail are given in miles (mi) with kilometers (km) in parenthesis. One mile = 1.609 km. The distances are approximate, as measured by a bike computer (odometer) which can be hard to keep running on a tough trail. Elevations in ft (m) are sometimes given in the descriptions, and the trail elevations can also be seen on the trail map. One m = 3.281 ft. Probably the most important function of the description is to explain clearly

Mountain biking clinics are a great method of advancing your skill level.

what should be done when there is a choice, such as at a trail junction or intersection. Hopefully I have done that, although there are certainly branching trails I have missed, so there will be times when your judgement will be needed.

The trail maps deserve some discussion. They were computer produced by combining elevation, water, road and photographic information obtained from various public agencies and commercial companies. GPS readings taken on several of the rides helped locate and map trail positions. The GPS readings were taken after the U.S. government removed the military jitter from the satellites, which supposedly makes readings accurate to 65 ft (20 m). On some rides that I have not ridden with a GPS, I mention in the ride description that the route shown in the map may differ from the actual trail position.

Each map is printed in the guide at a scale to show the complete ride. On each map there is a 1 km (.62 mi) spaced grid (on a couple of the maps a 2 km spaced grid is used), so distance can be estimated. You can cover considerable distance on a mountain bike, and my experience has indicated that you can also get WAY lost. Whatever you may think of technology, we have entered an age when GPS can determine position even in the most remote areas, and I have made it possible to use it if you want.

The map grid is drawn to fit Universal Transverse Mercator (UTM) Zone 18 NAD27 coordinates. In the mapping world, UTM is a projection method, Zone 18 is the slice of the earth's surface that includes New York, and NAD27 is the datum. A datum is a ellipsoid model of the earth, which is not a perfect sphere. The 1927 datum is commonly used in New York. You may also find maps or photographs using the 1983 (NAD83) datum; coordinates in this datum will not match those from NAD27, the difference being an offset of 25 to 250 m.

You do not need to know all these mapping particulars to use a GPS unit on your rides, just set it (or have the dealer set it) to display coordinates in UTM Zone 18 NAD27, distance in meters, elevation in meters. Take a look at the example map and notice the strange looking numbers on the vertical and horizontal lines, e.g. ^{5}18 and ^{48}97. These numbers are in a mapping notation, the ^{5}18 means the vertical line is 518 km or 518,000 m (the x-coordinate) east of a reference line. For zone 18, I believe the reference line goes through Indiana. Similarly, the horizontal line with ^{48}97 on it is 4897 km or 4,897,000 m (the y-coordinate) north of the reference line, the equator. So, with your GPS properly set, if you can receive enough satellites to get a reading and that reading is 518000, 4897000 you are right where the two lines cross. Of course, such easy to locate numbers never occur. The reading will be messy, like 517421, 4897627, so you have to interpolate. Larger numbers on the x-coordinate move you to the right, and larger values on the y-coordinate move you up. I have drawn a spot on the map at 517421,4897627; see if you agree with its location. If so, you're ready to go.

As with all technology, there are limitations to GPS. They do not work well under heavy tree cover, and in the summer you usually need to find a small opening to get a reading. The front display on most units usually shows what satellites are being received. You generally need at least three, and accuracy is best if they are widely scattered in the sky. In my experience good readings are most difficult to get in valleys, because some of the satellite signals are blocked

Example Map

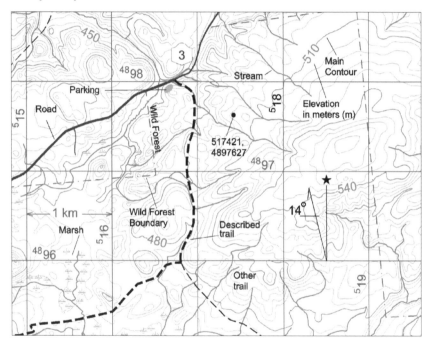

and you get readings only from the few directly overhead. Conversely, on the bare top of a mountain you will get great readings, unfortunately you are usually not lost in that situation. GPS units also have elevation outputs, but readings are not accurate unless signals are being received from 4 to 6 satellites, which you rarely get while submerged in the Adirondack forest. So if you want to know your elevation, use the barometric altimeter.

If you use a GPS unit, take a reading at the trailhead; it can help you get home if you become completely lost. If you forget to take this reading, but have the ride description with you, the trailhead coordinates are listed. With this reading, no matter how confused you become, an estimate of the distance and direction back to where you started can be made. Also check the elevation reading of the GPS unit at the trailhead. If it differs from the true elevation by more than 100 m, I manually set it to the correct value. The correct trailhead elevation is listed in the ride description and it can be estimated from the map contours (see below). If you use a barometric altimeter, it also needs setting at the correct trailhead value.

The traditional USGS 7.5 and 15 minute quad maps, and the newer 7.5 x 15 minute quad maps for NY use UTM Zone 18 NAD27; you can see the numbers printed along the edge of the map. These USGS prints also have latitude/longitude and New York State East Zone markings on them, however these two coordinate systems are not used in the guide.

The maps have elevation contours on them, with thicker lined main contours every 30 m (about 100 ft) and thin lined secondary contours at 6 m (about 20 ft). In some cases where trails go through fairly level terrain I have used 15 m main contours. These contours are helpful for position location if you use a barometric altimeter. The main contours are occasionally labeled with their elevation in meters.

A compass will read about 14 degrees off from true north throughout the Adirondacks. A true north/magnetic north arrow is shown on each map to remind you of this discrepancy. When using a compass, don't rotate it so the north seeking arrow lines up with the big "N" on the outside rim. Instead, make the arrow line up near the 346 degree point on the compass rim, and then rim N, E, S and W direction will point correctly.

Roads are shown by solid lines on the map. When it is near the trail, the Wild Forest boundary is shown by a dash-dash-dot line, usually with a label to indicate which side of the line is Wild Forest. Trails are shown with the mapping standard dashed line. The described trail is displayed with a wide line style to make it easily visible. Other adjoining and intersecting trails are shown as narrower lines. For each ride, I have ridden the bold described trail at least once, and sometimes a half dozen times. However, in many instances I have not ridden the adjacent trails; these were often just placed as you see them on historical maps. You may wish to try riding the side trails. Feel free to do so, but understand that their existence/location/condition is uncertain. That's enough, let's go ride!

southeast

The southeastern region of the park is closest to the Capital District (Albany, Schenectady, ...) Fortunately for residents of this area, it has two large wild forest areas, Lake George and Wilcox Lake. Both wild forests have numerous hiking trails, snowmobile trails and old roads. All of these have excellent riding. The Lake George wild forest can conveniently be divided into two areas, one east and the other west of the lake, since access to the two areas is so different. The east side of the lake has some technically challenging expert trails, with climbs and drops approaching 1600 ft (490 m). There is also some less difficult intermediate riding, and one beginner ride on the old jeep trail along the shore of the lake which, unfortunately, can be reached only after climbing Shelving Rock Mountain and descending to the shore. There is also a short beginner ride from the Hogtown trailhead to Dacy Clearing. One ride on the east side of the lake is described here.

The western part of the Lake George wild forest includes Tongue Mountain and a section north of Highway 9N. Like its companion area to the east, Tongue Mountain has challenging advanced terrain with some large elevation changes. Because of its excellent views and closeness to the Capital District, Tongue Mountain has considerable hiking traffic; be prepared to watch closely and yield the trail when riding here. It is not a good place to ride on major holiday weekends. Do not try to ride the Tongue Mountain crest from Fifth Peak to Montcalm Point. There are many very steep sections you will either have to lower your bike down or carry up. One ride along the shore of the mountain is described in this guide.

The northern area of the Lake George wild forest around Beech Mountain, Round and Buttermilk Ponds includes some old roads which offer enjoyable and less demanding riding. There appears to be little hiking on these trails. This section includes a ride on one of the roads.

The Wilcox Lake wild forest is more or less one piece of land, but it also has widely separated access points on the east and west sides. The eastern part around Harrisburg and Baldwin Springs has a number of wet, rocky, slippery, challenging and often frustrating snowmobile trails. There are also a couple of easy rides, and one on the Harrisburg road is described in this book.

The western part around Hope Falls, Wilcox Lake, Willis Lake and the Pine Orchard also has numerous snowmobile trails, is drier and generally less slippery than those trails around Harrisburg and Baldwin Springs. Riding is great here, and no less than four rides are described.

I have also included the Vanderwhacker Mountain Wild Forest in the southeastern section. There are two rides in this area that are described. One of these, the Irishtown ride, is an expert rated challenge, but the other into Stony Pond is much easier.

Stony Pond
Beginner

Distance:	**4.2 mi (6.8 km) out and back**
Difficulty:	**Easy intermediate/beginner**
Fitness Required:	**Low**
Climbing Required:	**200 ft (60 m)**
Time to ride:	**1 to 2 hours**
Wild Forest:	**Vanderwhacker Mountain**

General

This is an easy summer or fall afternoon ride. It is slightly more difficult than beginner, and would be a good ride for a beginner wanting to learn new skills. Stony Pond is a scenic destination. If you wish, this ride can be extended into something much more challenging.

Trail Access

The trailhead is on the east side on NY 28N, 3.9 mi north of the intersection of 28N and the Olmstedville Road (AP Morse Memorial highway) in Minerva. There is parking along the east side of the road. The elevation here is 2000 ft (610 m) and the coordinates are 579060, 4853555.

Description

From the trailhead, start riding east on an old road. The road surface is solid, with some rocks in it, easy intermediate, with some ups and downs. At 0.8 mi (1.29 km) and 1.0 (1.61) brooks are crossed; there is corduroy in the trail at the crossings. At 1.8 (2.90), there may be a long muddy spot with a lot of logs in it, probably not rideable. After the wet spot the trail returns to a road which occasionally narrows down to singletrack and then back to road width. At 2.1 (3.38) the leanto at Stony Pond is reached. For the described ride, return by the same route.

As mentioned, it is possible to extend this ride. From the Stony Pond leanto, there is a trail going south to Little and Big Sherman Ponds and then drops to Long Hill Road at Irishtown. The section to the Sherman Ponds is singletrack and more difficult than the road into Stony Pond. At the time of this writing, I have not ridden the section from the ponds on down. If that is ridden, turn right (south) on Long Hill road, ride to the Olmstedville Road, turn right again and ride to highway 28N. Making one more right turn, ride back to the trailhead.

For a second alternative, from the Stony Pond leanto, there is also a trail going north to Center Pond, Barnes Pond and then to Hewitt Pond. The trail going north is narrow, starting off intermediate and eventually becoming advanced, with some difficult drops and climbs. The drop to Barnes Pond is a real challenge. After some additional climbing and descending the trail ends on the road into the Hewitt Club; at this road turn left to get back to 28N, then turn left (south) again to ride back to the trailhead.

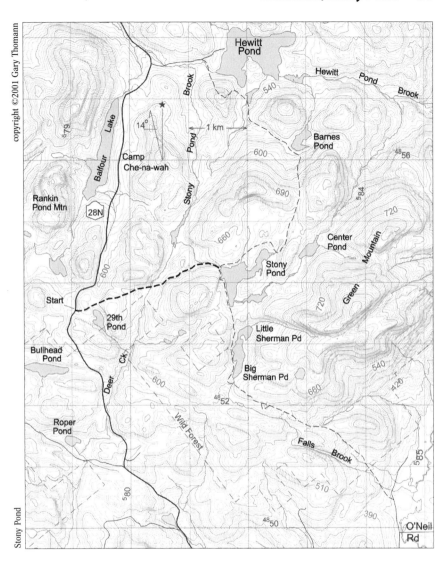

Stony Pond

Harrisburg Lake to Bakertown Bridge
Beginner

Distance: 8.74 mi (14.06 km) in and out

Difficulty: Beginner

Climbing: 530 ft (160 m)

Time to ride: 1 - 2 hours

Wild Forest: Wilcox Lake (eastern access)

General

This trail provides scenery along East Stony Creek and even gives you a chance to lift your head and view it; you ride a dirt road with a only few rocks and some mud holes to watch for. The road becomes more eroded the further you get from Harrisburg Lake. There are a few buildings along the road and you might meet one or two vehicles. Extra distance on more challenging trails can be added from the turnaround point at the Bakertown bridge, or by riding north on the Arrow trail.

Trail Access

Finding the trailhead is somewhat of an adventure in itself. Directions will be given from the village of Lake Luzerne, which you can get to from I87 by taking 9N south from Exit 21. From 9N in Lake Lucerne at the intersection which has a Stewarts store on the corner, go west on Bay Road, then at .45 mi turn left on Bridge Street, which is also highway 4. At .85 mi turn right on Saratoga County highway 1, which I believe is also called Stony Creek Road.

At 7.4 mi you cross into Warren County, and the highway 1 marker will no longer be seen. At 10.5 you come into the village of Stony Creek. Drive across Roaring Branch Rd and keep right on going. Notice the Stony Creek Inn will be on your left. It serves Mexican food on Sundays, making that a good day to do the ride. Continuing down the road you will see a "Deadend 11 mi" sign, drive on. At 15.85 mi Wolf Pond Rd goes off to the right, continue straight ahead passing through the village of Knowelhurst. At 21.1 mi drive past the Harrisburg Resort on the left, and at 21.6 mi park in the lot on the right where there is a DEC registration box. The parking lot elevation is 1495 ft (456 m) and the coordinates are 574345, 4806000. If you made it to here, the rest is easy.

Description

In the parking lot there is a sign stating 2.3 mi to the Arrow Trail and 5.3 mi to Wilcox Lake. For the described ride you will turnaround at 4.37 mi, still a little ways from Wilcox Lake. Start riding west. At 0.2 mi (.32 km) cross Harrisburg Lake on a small bridge and begin climbing on a driveable road. At .60 (.97) there is a road going off to the left; continue straight. At 1.05 (1.69) you reach the top of the climb; there are a couple of trails going off to the right. Ignore them and continue west on the road and start descending. At 1.34 (2.16) there is a trailer on the left and then a camp on the left at 1.44 (2.32). Then you begin to climb again and enter public land. At 1.69 (2.72) there is a road going off to the right; bypass it and continue west. You begin a long descent with one short climbing section in it and at 2.41 (3.89) the Arrow trail goes off to the right; for the described ride continue on. At 2.73 (4.40) there is a rideable suspension bridge over the creek, but you may want to check the bridge boards for rot before you go charging across.

After the bridge the road is a little more difficult, dirt surface with a few rocks and probably some mud puddles to ride around. It is still beginner, but more interesting to ride. Just after the bridge there is a trail up to the left which goes to a fire circle; just continue down the road. At 3.09 (4.97) Bakertown appears on your left. You are entering a small section of private land. At 4.05 (6.52) there is a small overlook on the right next to East Stony Creek, with one sign listing the distance back to Harrisburg Lake, and another listing distances for destinations ahead (Bakertown bridge, Wilcox Lake, Willis Lake and Brownell Camp). At 4.26 (6.86) there may be a camp on the left and the Bakertown sus-

Rock paving in a wet section of trail.

pension bridge over East Stony Creek appears at 4.37 (7.03).

At the bridge, for the easy described ride turn around and ride back to the trailhead. If you are not yet tired (or don't believe you will finish tired enough if you just turn around and ride back), you can ride on south toward Brownell Camp along the side of the creek, as described else-where in the guide. Another alternative is to cross the suspension bridge, do the tough climb up to the T intersection at the top and turn right to drop down to Wilcox Lake or left toward Willis Lake/Pumpkin Hollow. The trail from Pumpkin Hollow to Wilcox Lake is also described in the guide. Finally, a last alternative is on the way back to venture up the Arrow trail a ways. I have ridden the Arrow trail, but do not describe it in the guide. I believe you will find it challenging.

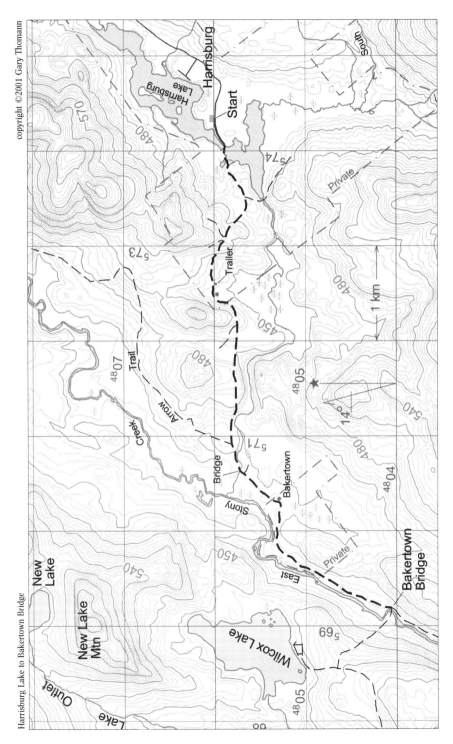

Harrisburg Lake to Bakertown Bridge

3

Pumpkin Hollow to the Pine Orchard
Beginner/Intermediate

Distance: 11.9 mi (19.2 km), in and out

Difficulty: Beginner and Intermediate

Climbing: 1150 ft (350 m)

Time to ride: 3 to 5 hours

Wild Forest: Wilcox Lake (western access)

General

The Pine Orchard contains old growth trees, both scenic and awesome. You ride to the orchard on a snowmobile trail of variable difficulty, beginner and intermediate with a couple of short expert sections. If desired, a second trail access can be used for a shorter less strenuous ride. Part of the return trip can be done on regular roads if desired.

Trail Access

The ride begins at the Pumpkin Hollow trailhead; from NY 30, 4.1 mi south of the Wells town hall turn east on Pumpkin Hollow Road. There is a large white building on the east side of the highway just north of the turn. Drive 1.7 mi to the trailhead, climbing about 350 ft (105 m). There is parking on the north side of the road. The elevation at the parking area is 1280 ft (390 m) and the coordinates are 560890, 4802055.

To reach the alternate trail access, from Highway 30 in the northern part of Wells, just south of the bridge across Algonquin Lake, turn east on Griffin road. Go .81 mi and turn right on Windfall Road. Go another 1.0 mi and turn right on Dorr/Flater road, which is gravel. Go 2.0 mi on Dorr road and park in the lot on the right before you come to the Flater's property. The elevation here is 1515 ft (462 m) and the coordinates are 562275, 4806540. Ride past the Flater house and continue to the trail junction, which will be at the 3.94 mi (6.34 km) point of the description below.

Description

At the Pumpkin Hollow trailhead a sign points north stating it is 5 mi to the Pine Orchard, a slight underestimate of the actual distance. Start riding north on a wide trail, which will swing east then back north and cross the Willis Lake outlet. The trail then goes west and finally back north again at about .37 mi (.6 km). It is about 6 ft wide with probably a pine needle/dirt surface; few rocks, beginner rated except for all the roots knitting the surface. At .87 (1.4) a gentle climb will start, and there will be more rocks, but fewer roots in the trail.

About 1.0 (1.6) you will see a small stream on the left, and shortly the trail drops down to cross the stream at a rocky crossing which may be rideable if you are aggressive. After crossing the stream the trail swings left then right to climb on a switchback and at 1.16 (1.86) a small creek is crossed via a wooden bridge. The beginner rated trail continues through the hardwood/softwood forest, and then about 1.40 (2.25) there is an intermediate rated rock garden about 150 ft (45 m) long. The trail continues, with the terrain gently dropping on the left and rising on the right. Then rocks become more numerous increasing the trail difficulty, and at 1.57 (2.53) there is a section of rock wall on the left (west) edge of the trail.

After the rock wall, descend to what will probably be a wet spot, then do a short climb and continue on an easy bench cut trail. Notice Coulombe Creek off to the left. At 1.92 (3.09) the trail crosses the creek on a wooden bridge. The rocks before and after the bridge make for a challenging crossing; try it if you wish. Now begins the most challenging part of this ride, as you climb a rocky trail, intermediate or perhaps even expert rated. The tough climb lasts for about .31 mi (.50 km) and then the trail is easier, although still climbing.

A junction is reached at 2.59 (4.16) alongside a small stream. The elevation here is about 1215 ft (370 m). For the described ride, make a right turn (the trail straight ahead drops down to highway 30). Just beyond the turn there is a neat rock garden to ride. Then the trail is easier again, with some ups, downs, and (probably) damp spots.

Next there is a nice easy drop to 3.03 (4.87) and then a wet spot with an old decayed pallet bridge across it. After the bridge the trail angles left and climbs slightly, and you ride an easy trail section, interrupted by a short steep climb at 3.19 (5.13), after which you make a right turn (there is an arrow directing you to turn). Continue climbing. At 3.26 (5.25) there is big rock formation on the right, and at 3.32 (5.34) reach the top, where the trail surface is rock. The elevation here is 1560 ft (475 m).

Now the trail starts to drop. An arrow directs you to turn right, after which you descend steeply. This drop is easily ridden because the trail surface is smooth. The trail turns back to the north and becomes tough and rocky. At 3.46 (5.57) there are two large boulders, one on each side of the trail. I suspect they are erratics. The trail continues to gently descend, although there is one sharp little 10 ft climb.

Three riders emerge from the fog on this beginner trail.

At 3.71 (5.97), where there is a sign on a tree, the trail enters private land, and there is a rocky expert section. A junction is reached at 3.94 (6.34). Coming in from the left is the alternate entrance for this ride. Pointing back the way you came is a sign stating it is 2.6 mi back to Willis Lake Rd, a rather low estimate compared to the 3.94 I measured. For the assigned ride, continue riding north.

The trail changes to beginner rated, descending gently on a smooth wide road, with an occasional rock. At 4.58 (7.37) ride across a bridge over a small stream that is a Mill Creek tributary. This small stream probably has a local name I am unaware of. The trail remains beginner. At 5.36 (8.63) there is a rocky stream on the right, and then the trail begins to climb. At about 5.43

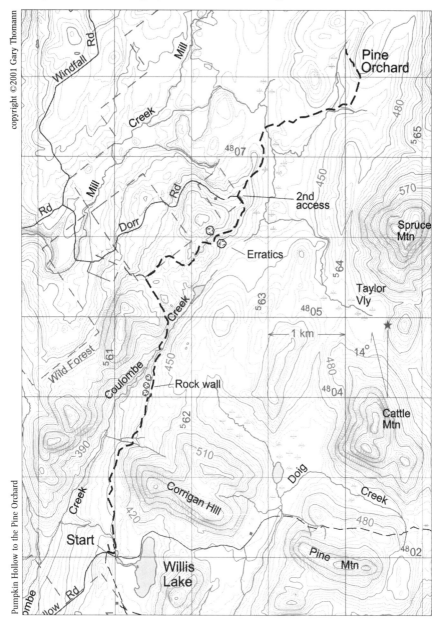

(8.74) you will see the first of the big pines. At 5.79 (9.08) there is a Pine Orchard sign tacked to a tree. Continue through the Pine Orchard and at 5.97 (9.60) the trail drops down to a marshy area. Although the trail continues north, in my experience it is rather poorly defined, and discretion would indicate you turn around.

On the return trip, there will be a fast enjoyable downhill from the Pine Orchard back to the Mill Creek tributary; if you are riding on a weekend (anytime, actually) watch out for hikers. When you get back to the junction, you have a choice of the return route; either the same route you rode in on, or ride down (west) on Dorr Rd, make a left turn onto Windfall Road, then left on Griffin Road and continue to Highway 30. Turn left (south) on the highway and ride about 4.6 miles to Pumpkin Hollow Rd, turn left (east) and ride up the hill to the Pumpkin Hollow trailhead.

4

Pumpkin Hollow to Wilcox Lake
Beginner/Intermediate

Distance: 22.2 km (13.8 mi), in and out

Difficulty: Intermediate with a couple of expert sections

Climbing: 350 m (1150 ft)

Time to ride: 3 to 5 hours

Wild Forest: Wilcox Lake (western access)

General

The Pumpkin Hollow trailhead is a great starting point, and three rides are described from it. For this second ride, the destination is the leanto on scenic Wilcox Lake, where you can take a swim. The trail is a double/singletrack snowmobile trail with rideable descents, some climbs that will have to be walked, and some very rocky stream crossings. This trail can also be used as part of a larger and challenging loop ride by connecting it with some of the other rides discussed in this section.

Trail Access

To get to the Pumpkin Hollow trailhead, from NY highway 30, 4.1 mi south of the Wells town hall, turn east on Pumpkin Hollow Road. There is a large white building on the east side of the highway just north of the turn. Drive 1.7 mi to the trailhead, climbing about 350 ft (105 m). There is parking on the north side of the road. The elevation at the parking area is 1280 ft (390 m) and the coordinates are 560890, 4802055.

Description

Start riding east on the hard surfaced road. The Willis Lake outlet is crossed at .07 mi (.11 km), and the lake appears on the south side of the road, along with several houses and camps in a section of privately owned land. At .25 (.41) the road changes to gravel. At 1.43 (2.30) there is a camp on the left in another privately owned section, at the edge of which is a DEC sign posted on a tree. The sign states it is 4.9 mi to Wilcox Lake and 10.0 mi to Harrisburg.

At 1.8 (2.9) the driveable road ends at a barrier. Ride around it and cross Doig Creek on a wooden bridge. Then on a wide dirt/grass trail, begin a climb which may be difficult to ride if you haven't yet warmed up. Near the bottom of the climb there is a trail that goes to the left (north); ignore this diversion and continue east. On your left you will notice a small stream flowing back down to Doig Creek. The climb becomes easier for a while and then, just after crossing a minute stream flowing right to left, there is a more difficult climb, probably too steep to ride. In the middle of this more difficult section are some log steps/corduroy which are very slick when wet, a fact to remember for the return trip. The top of the difficult climb is reached at about 2.3 (3.7), at 1575 ft (480 m) elevation.

The trail becomes a little narrower, still a couple of meters wide, probably covered with pine needles, with a few rocks and roots. It is nice riding, not very difficult. The trail drops down slightly and then resumes climbing. At 2.4 (3.86) there is a fork; take the right fork, although the left fork will also come back to the main trail a little later. At 3.0 (4.8) the climbing ends at an elevation of 1625 ft (495 m), and there is a long but not difficult descent, finishing at another encounter with Doig Creek, flowing right to left this time. Now, instead of a bridge, rock sentinels guard the crossing and you may wish to walk across.

The trail gradually becomes more difficult as rocks and roots become more numerous. There are two more rocky stream crossings, which you can attempt if you like rock gardens. The second crossing is reached after a short drop. At 3.9 (6.3) an expert rated rocky drop is reached, rideable with some slick maneuvering. After the drop the enjoyable rocky trail continues with, I believe, five small stream crossings, each again having well guarded rocky crossings. At 5.3 (8.5), the bridge over Wilcox Lake outlet is reached, just after a large rock garden.

Now the trail abruptly turns left (north), and it is not well marked. After

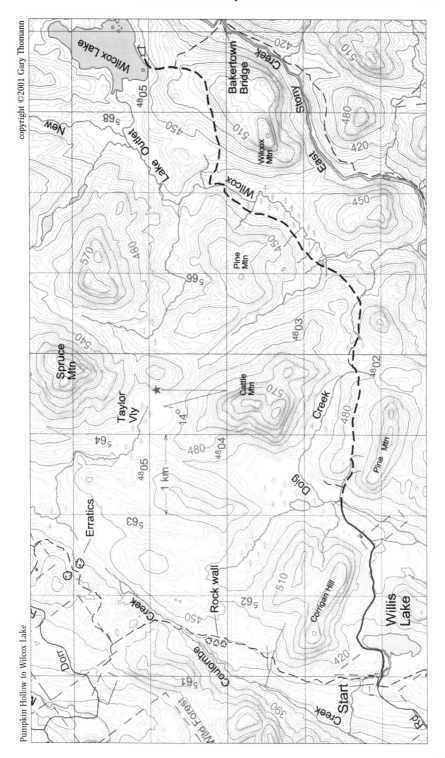

Pumpkin Hollow to Wilcox Lake

going about 100 m north, the trail turns east again and begins a 360 ft (110 m) climb to the shoulder of Wilcox Mountain. You will probably have to walk some of this ascent. The top of the shoulder is reached at 6.2 (10.0) followed by an enjoyable descent to a trail junction at 6.5 (10.5).

At this junction, the trail to the southeast (right) begins an expert rated descent to the Bakertown Bridge over East Stony Creek. (After the creek crossing the trail to the north goes to Harrisburg and the one to the south to Hope Falls, rides described elsewhere in the guide). For the described ride, take the left turn (going north); a steep but rideable drop to Wilcox Lake. At the lake shore, go east a short distance to the leanto, reached at 6.9 (11.1), a good spot for lunch or a snack. The return to the Pumpkin Hollow trailhead is by the same route.

5

Beech Mountain/Blackberry Alley
Intermediate

Distance: 8.3 mi (13.4 km) for the out and back ride

Difficulty: Intermediate

Climbing Required: 1300 ft (396 m)

Time to ride: 3 to 4 hours

Wild Forest: Lake George (west side)

General

This ride is on an old road north of highway 9N. It has some badly washed out sections and some large rock ledges that make fine ingredients for mountain bike cuisine. The road is completely rideable (for good climbers) except for one climb and a couple of bridges. It is a good ride for wet spring conditions and holiday weekends. The road surface is hard and there is not a lot of hiking on it. The ride is out and back with a short loop at the far end. This loop briefly goes onto private land.

Trail Access

Take Exit 24 from the Northway (I87) and drive east 5 mi to North Bolton, then turn north on NY 9N. At 9.4 mi (4.4 mi after turning north), the Clay Meadows trailhead will appear on the right; keep driving north and at 10.7 mi continue straight on a Wardsboro Road when 9N turns to the right. At 12.0 mi, just after the road crosses Bay Brook, take a right turn and drive east. At 14.1 mi there is a house on the left and the road begins to deteriorate and climb. A little past the house, park in the small space on the right which has room for 3 or 4 cars. Do not block the road with the parked car(s). The elevation at this point is 590 ft (180 m) and coordinates are 613370, 4838430.

Description

Start riding north/northeast; the road begins to climb immediately. The first 1.4 mi (2.25 km) is a dirt road wide enough for vehicles, rated easy intermediate with some rocks. There may be some wet areas. At 0.6 (.97) there is a dead-end trail going off to the left, continue straight. At 0.7 (1.13) there is a camp on the right. Just after the camp the road enters Wild Forest classified land. At 1.2 (1.93) there is an old damaged bridge which cannot be ridden, although it is possible to ride around the bridge on the left. Right after the bridge the trail splits for a short distance; the left fork is the toughest. At 1.4 (2.25), the elevation is 1200 ft (366 m), 600 ft (183 m) above the trailhead.

There is a tough climb starting at 1.4 (2.25) with several rock ledges in it; the ledges are especially difficult to ride if wet. The trail is then less steep for a distance, but from about 2.0 (3.22) to 2.2 (3.54) there is an ascent that is a test of fitness and climbing skills. Next there is an easy intermediate slightly downhill section and a small creek is crossed at 2.5 (4.02). Scout the bridge over this creek; it may be very slippery. It is possible to ride through the stream on the left side of the bridge. After crossing the creek, the road continues level with an easy intermediate to intermediate rating.

At 2.9 (4.67) the trail splits - take the right fork; later the described ride will come back down the left fork. Just past the fork is a tough but rideable climb. At 3.0 (4.83) there is a beaver pond on the left.. At 3.5 (5.63) there is a tough intermediate rated, but rideable climb about 0.2 mi (.32 km) long, with a difficult ledge right at the top to finish you off. At the top of this climb the elevation is just under 1700 ft (518 m), about 1100 ft (335 m) above the start. Next, beginning at 3.7 (5.95), there is a fairly steep technical downhill section which drops 200 ft (61 m). There are lots of rocks on this section, and in the summer and fall blackberry bush branches hang across the trail. You can choose your route to avoid the larger rocks or the thorns, but probably not both. Just after the descent begins the trail enters private land. Respect any Posted or No Trespassing signs that you encounter. If the trail is closed you

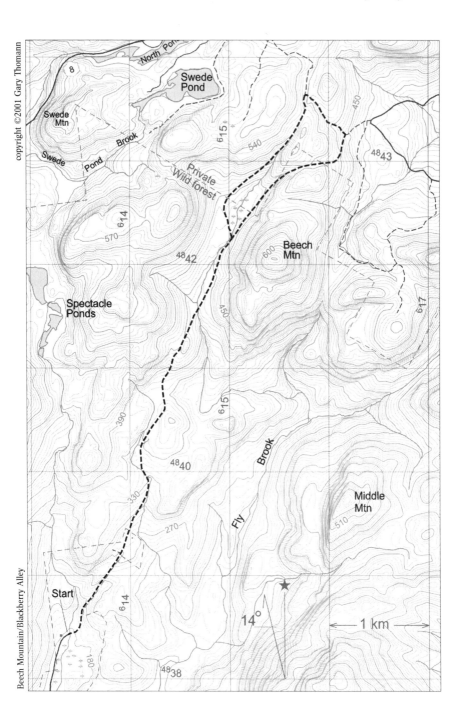

should ride back to the trailhead the same way you came in.

At 4.0 (6.44) is a T junction at the bottom of the descent. The trail to the right (northeast) goes over to Split Rock Road. For the ride described here, take the left turn. After the turn, there is a very difficult ascent up a rocky road/stream bed that can be ridden only by a phenomenal climber, maybe John Tomac on his best day. The top of this climb is reached at 4.4 (7.08), again at 1700 ft (518 m) elevation, at another T intersection. The trail to the right leads to Swede Pond and/or Graphite. For this ride, take the left turn onto a trail going back southwest and roughly parallel to the trail ridden earlier. This trail is wet and grassy, and it may be difficult to see the rocks in the road because of the grass. In the summer and fall there are also more blackberry branches. The trail re-enters Wild Forest land. At 5.4 (8.69) there may be a short detour around a section of the trail a beaver dam has flooded and then the trail crosses a small stream that is rideable if approached with enough speed. At 5.5 (8.85) you arrive back at the trail junction that was originally reached at 2.9 (4.67).

The ride now returns to the cars on the same trail ridden earlier. At the junction the elevation is just above 1400 ft (427 m), so you have mountain bike dollars to spend, 800 English or 245 Metric . Be careful not to ride at a speed way above your ability The cars are reached at 8.3 mi (13.4 km).

6

Brownell Camp to Bakertown Bridge
Intermediate/Expert

Distance: 8.27 mi (13.3 km) in and out

Difficulty: Intermediate & expert

Climbing: 490 ft (150 m)

Time to ride: 2 to 4 hours

Wild Forest: Wilcox Lake (western access)

General

This ride runs alongside East Stony Creek, a small fast moving river full of boulders and rapids. If you overheat, there are many opportunities to jump into the cool water. On the trail, you will enjoy expert rated rock gardens and some very challenging small creek crossings. There will also be some wet areas. There are various options to add distance to this ride.

Trail Access

The ride begins at the parking lot near Brownell Camp. From highway 30, about 8.4 mi south of the Wells town hall, turn east on Creek Road and drive 2.8 mi until you cross East Stony Creek and dead end at a T intersection. To the right (south) is Hope Falls Rd. Don't go there. Turn left (north) and follow the road along the east side of the creek. This road may be named Mud Creek Road, although the name doesn't matter. 3.55 mi after starting north the road will change from hard surface to gravel and at 4.9 mi will end at a small parking lot right next to the creek. Park here. The parking lot elevation is 1100 ft (335 m) and the coordinates are 566100, 4799790.

As an alternate way to the trailhead, from the Village of Northville on Main Street just a few hundred feet north of the Grand Union grocery store set your trip odometer to 0.0 and turn west on Reed Street, which as you drive along will change to Old Northville Road. At 3.05 mi turn right on Hope Falls Rd; the road sign looks like something from an old trading post or cigar store. Drive north until you register 5.65 mi, where Creek road will come in from the left. Continue north as described in the previous paragraph.

Description

The trail starts north right along the creek, about 5 or 6 ft wide and easy. There is a sign-in box a few feet down the trail. There are some planks laid down on the trail to help get across wet areas. The trail has orange snowmobile and blue hiking markers. At .15 mi (.24 km) there is a bridge over Tenant Creek. It is difficult to ride the bridge going north because of the large step up onto the bridge; coming back south it is much easier to ride across.

The trail leaves the creek at around .37 (.60) and begins to climb, staying technically easy. At .55 (.89) there is a wet spot, with what I will call a plank bridge across it. The bridge consists of 2 x 6 planks about 2 ft long nailed across beams parallel to the trail. The plank bridge is easily rideable when dry, although when wet it will be slick. After the bridge the trail stays technically beginner with several small descents and climbs, which are rideable but require some strength. Around .79 (1.27) a few more rocks start to appear in the trail, and at .99 (1.59) there is another plank bridge. East Stony Creek is to the west, but not in sight.

The fun (or difficulty) begins when you enter a hundred foot long wet expert rated rock garden. Ride as much of it as you can. At 1.16 (1.86) there is another plank bridge; the elevation at this point is 1198 ft (365 m). The trail comes back alongside the creek at 1.24 (2.0), and becomes easy to ride, with a couple of intermediate rated rock sections. At 1.45 (2.33) you come to the first of the small stream crossings, an unnamed stream channel only a few feet wide, but also a few feet deep. It has several rocks in it (one of which has a root snaking across it). Try to ride across if you want.

At 1.52 (2.44) there is a long expert rock garden on an uphill section that is very difficult to ride in this direction; you may be able to ride it on the way back. After about 400 ft the rocks become easier for a while, intermediate rated. And then, at 1.65 (2.65) there are two of the small stream crossings, about 20 ft apart. Again, try to ride them if you want (dare); the first one is particularly challenging. After the crossings the trail continues rocky, expert and intermediate rated.

At 1.75 (2.82) there is another small stream crossing that is probably rideable if you charge it. The trail continues rocky and intermediate and at 1.90 (3.06) there is a wider stream crossing. Although I could be proved wrong, I believe this crossing is unrideable. After this crossing, the trail is easier, leaves the

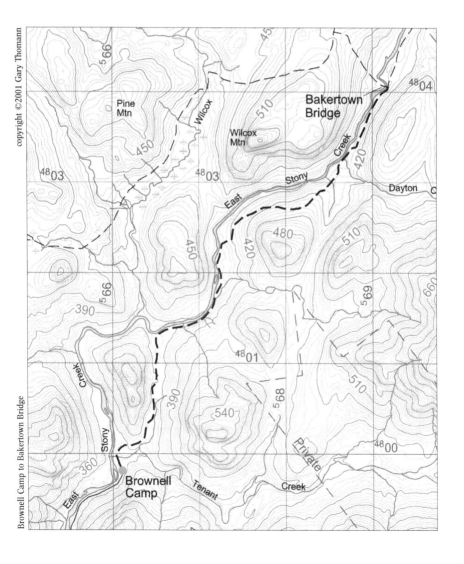

Brownell Camp to Bakertown Bridge

creek for a short while, and drops back down to the creek at 2.32 (3.74). There is an intermediate but challenging rocky section, and at about 2.54 (4.09) the trail begins to ascend and diverges from the creek. The climbing, doable if you have the fitness, continues to about 3.00 (4.83), at which point the elevation is 1440 ft (440 m).

From the top, ride an easy descent that may be interrupted by a couple of wet sections. At 3.26 (5.25) there is a difficult to ride stream crossing and at 3.47 (5.58) the trail comes back to East Stony Creek at the point where Dayton Creek flows into it. At one time there was a snowmobile bridge over Dayton Creek, but in Oct. of 2000 it was gone. Dayton Creek is wide and rocky and

A bridge crossing is the perfect time to catch a view...and a rest.

without the bridge probably not rideable.

After the Dayton Creek crossing the trail difficulty varies, rocky and intermediate/expert challenges interspersed with beginner sections. At 4.13 (6.65) the Bakertown Bridge over East Stony Creek is reached, and you have several choices. For the prescribed ride, return to the trailhead back the way you came in. On the return there will be more descending than ascending, and you should find many of the rock gardens easier to ride than they were before. If you wish to ride further, one option is to continue north along East Stony Creek, on the Harrisburg Road. It is beginner rated. (See the Harrisburg Lake to Bakertown Bridge description elsewhere in the guide.) Another option for a longer ride is to cross East Stony Creek on the Bakertown bridge and ride the ascending trail up to the trail junction and turn right to drop to Wilcox Lake or left to head toward the Pumpkin Hollow trailhead. For more information about these options, check the Pumpkin Hollow to Wilcox Lake ride description.

Lake George Northwest Bay Trail

Expert

Distance: 10.6 mi (17.1 km) out and back

Difficulty: Expert

Climbing Required: 400 ft (120 m), many short climbs and descents

Time to ride: 3 to 4 hours

Wild Forest: Lake George (western side)

General

Tongue Mountain is a rocky peninsula that juts into Lake George. This ride is along the shoreline of Tongue Mountain on a section of the lake named Northwest Bay. You ride from Clay Meadows to Montcalm Point, where there is a beautiful lake view. The ride is surprisingly challenging, considering there are no long climbs or descents, but several short ones 50 to 200 ft long. The trail has some singletrack, roots that are slippery when wet, occasional rocky sections, and a few tricky stream crossings. The trail is almost all rideable for expert riders, and less experienced riders can attempt if they walk some sections. The trail was originally constructed during the Depression by workers in the Civilian Conservation Corps (CCC) as a horse trail, and generally has a solid surface. Trailhead elevation is 413 ft (126 m) and the coordinates are 612240, 4831380.

Trail Access

This ride begins from the Clay Meadows trailhead on the west side of Lake George. Take Exit 24 off the Northway (I87) and drive east 5 mi to North

Bolton. Then go north 4.4 mi on NY 9N; the Clay Meadows trailhead is on the right. There is a small parking lot on the right just north of the trailhead, and a second parking area about 200 ft further north if the first one is full.

Description

Begin by riding east from the trailhead on a packed dirt surface covered by pine needles. There is a nice drop near the start, with lots of roots across the trail. There is a rideable plank bridge at 0.2 mi (.32 km). This first section of trail drops about 150 ft (93 m). At 0.4 (.64) there is a junction. The trail continuing east climbs to the crest of Tongue Mountain. But, for this ride, take a right turn onto a trail about 6 ft wide with a firm dirt surface, usually with a light covering of needles or leaves. There will be many rocks and roots and perhaps a few wet spots. Considerable rock work along the edge of the trail can be seen. Right after starting south there is a short rideable bridge. At 0.9 (1.45) there is a steep but rideable climb, and then at 1.0 (1.61) a stream crossing with a gap that is tricky to ride; scouting is advised. There is a steep 200 ft (60 m) climb at 1.1 (1.77) that probably has to be walked. On the return trip, it is an enjoyable drop, not to be wasted by walking.

Next the trail drops towards the bay shore; here about 5 ft wide, dirt surfaced with lots of rocks and roots. At 1.7 (2.74) there is another tricky stream to ride. The lake (Northwest Bay) is reached at 2.3 (3.7) right after crossing a small bridge. The downhill section to the lake is intermediate and great fun.

Continue south along the bay shore, through several short 20 ft climbs and descents. At 2.4 (3.86) there is a sharp short drop. At 2.6 (4.18) a very sharp climb is followed by a sharp drop, at the bottom of which you go over a bridge. At 2.8 (4.50) there is a difficult advanced rocky section. At 3.2 (5.15) there is another difficult rocky stretch right along the lake shore, followed by a small campsite right on the bay edge. There is a stream crossing at 3.3 (5.31) that must be walked, followed by an extremely sharp 15 ft climb that cannot be ridden. Scout this drop before trying to ride down it on the way back. The trail continues singletrack with rocks and roots. The trail turns sharply right at 3.5 (5.63) over what appears to be a beaver dam. This turn is difficult to see.

There is a steep hard to ride climb at 4.1 (6.60), and then a sharp drop with a tough stream crossing at the bottom, followed by some roots and logs. At 4.4 (7.08) there is a wet section that may have to be walked, depending on recent precipitation. Shortly after this wet section the trail narrows to about a foot wide, bench cut into a slope that drops down to the lake. It's a good section to practice your balancing skills.

The trail narrows so at 4.7 (7.56) that it must be walked for a short distance. Immediately beyond, the trail goes left and climbs a rocky section. You will probably have to walk this section also. At 5.08 (8.18) there is a trail junction,

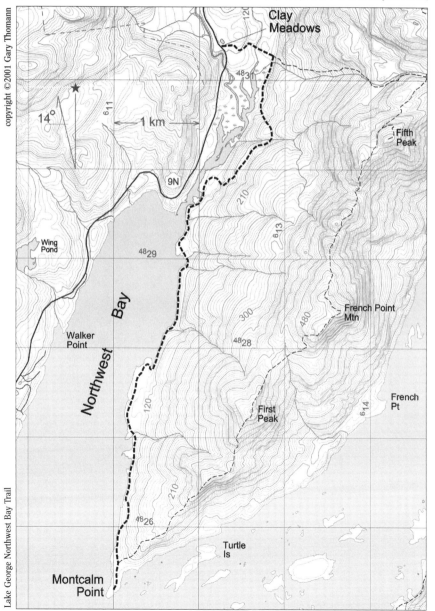

The expert class races through rocky terrain at Gore Mountain.

with a trail going off to the left, which climbs to the crest of Tongue Mountain; it is too steep to ride going north from this point. Just keep going straight. The tip of Montcalm Point is reached at 5.3 mi (8.53 km). After pausing for scenery, food and rest, ride back the same way.

8

Pumpkin Hollow to Creek Road
Expert

Distance: 7.1 mi (11.4 km) on the trail, 8.3 (13.3) on road return

Difficulty: Expert, or even better (worse)

Climbing: 330 ft (100 m) on the trail, 790 ft (240 m) road

Time to ride: 2 - 3 hours on the trail, 1 hr on the road

Wild Forest: Wilcox Lake (western access)

General

You will find adventure and scenery on this ride. The scenery is at Murphy lake, the adventure is continuous on this rocky trail that has above expert, expert and intermediate sections. It is technically much more difficult than the other two rides out of the Pumpkin Hollow trailhead. There are three very challenging rocky downhills, which you can bypass if you wish. If you have elbow and knee pads, this is a good time to wear them.

Trail Access

The ride begins at the Pumpkin Hollow trailhead; from NY 30 4.1 mi south of the Wells town hall turn east on Pumpkin Hollow Road. There is a large white building on the east side of the highway just north of the turn. Drive 1.7 mi to the trailhead, climbing about 350 ft (105 m). There is parking on the north side of the road. The elevation at the parking area is 1280 ft (390 m) and the coordinates are 560890, 4802055.

Description

On the trailhead sign, for the trail going south it states Murphy Lake is 4.0 mi, Middle Lake 4.5 and Bennett Lake 6.0. Start riding south on a beginner rated trail that has some rocks and roots. At .28 mi (.45 km) there is a 150 ft stretch of corduroy that is very slick and probably unrideable. At .43 (.69) there is a shack visible through the trees to the right. Then, shortly after there is a crossing trail; to the right and back it goes to the shack, I do not know where the branch left and forward goes. For this ride, continue south (actually going at about 140 degrees). At .56 (.90) there is a plank section that you may be able to ride, then for a few hundred feet there is a rocky and difficult section, followed by another plank bridge. The trail turns to the southwest, rocky, difficult, and probably wet. At about .89 (1.43) the trail angles back to the south; it is wide with a lot of roots here.

There is a plank bridge at .94 (1.51) that is difficult to ride, and a couple of metal poles which once must have been part of a gate. Then there is probably a wet spot followed by another of these plank bridges. Next the trail becomes a little easier to ride, turning to the east, with a nice intermediate rated drop ending at about 1.12 (1.93). The trail turns back south, slightly descending, and a rideable bridge over a creek approaches at 1.27 (2.05). The trail narrows but stays easily rideable and a bridge crosses Doig Creek at 1.45 (2.34). This bridge is more difficult to ride than the preceding one.

After the creek is a long rocky, rooty, tough but rideable climb. The grade levels some about 1.76 (2.83) and the top is reached at 1.95 (3.13). The elevation here is about 1310 ft (400 m), just slightly higher than the trailhead. The trail then meanders along the west edge of a marshy wet section. At 2.1 (3.38) cross a little bridge that suddenly ends with a drop-off. You can do a rear wheel drop off the bridge if such tricks are in your mountain bike folder.

Adjust your helmet and check that your shoes are tightly tied, you are going to be tested. For a couple hundred feet after the bridge it is expert rated rocky singletrack, after which it softens to intermediate, but still rocky and rooty. Around 2.34 (3.77) you may notice a small stream on your left, flowing back north. Then there is a difficult crossing of this stream, followed by a difficult rocky/rooty climb. Another small stream appears on the left, which drains Murphy Lake back into the marshy area just passed. The trail continues along the stream, going through a 300 foot long rock garden that is probably unrideable, then becomes easier, only expert/intermediate. At 2.83 (4.56) there is a very difficult, probably unrideable, crossing of this creek over to the east side. The trail continues along the east side of the creek, going up a rocky probably unrideable climb. It would be an expert rated drop riding the other direction. The trail continues rocky and at least expert. At 3.08 (5.70) Murphy Lake is reached. The trail turns east to bump along the northern and eastern sides of the lake; it is expert rated singletrack. At 3.78 (6.09) the trail swings up and over a little knoll to the Murphy Lake Leanto. The elevation here is about 1475 ft (450 m), well above that of the trailhead. You can sit in the leanto, eat and drink a little, and maybe dream about how next time you will ride the trail clean.

Continuing from the leanto are more rocky experiences, and some sweet downhills. To get you started again, the trail starts out beginner, with

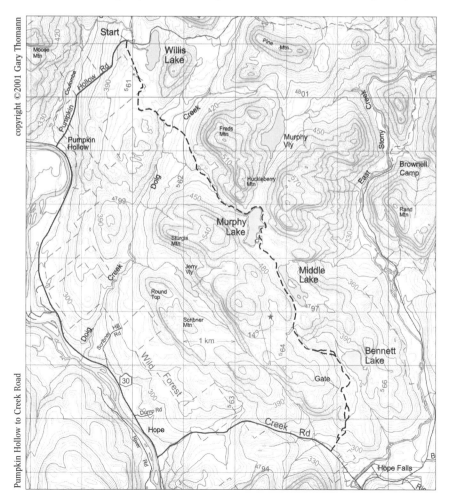

occasional intermediate sections. Around 4.15 (6.67) an easy drop starts, at the bottom of which is an intermediate rock garden, followed by a second rock garden a little further along. About 4.38 (7.04) you can see Middle Lake on the left, and the trail continues along the lake, beginner/intermediate here. After leaving the lake the trail drops again, rocky and intermediate. A small stream is crossed at 5.03 (8.10), following which the trail continues to drop, first intermediate then becoming easier.

At 5.3 (8.89) there is a trail off to the left, and here is the first of three steep rocky downhills you can either ride or bypass. Your decision is dependent on how much you like rocks, or maybe on how much common sense you have. For this first drop, the left is the easy route and straight ahead is the rocky way. Stand at the top, look down the drop, and decide if you want to attempt it. The two routes rejoin about 600 ft later.

After this drop, there is a somewhat easier intermediate/expert drop after which the surface becomes easier and the trail turns to the west. There is a barrier with a swinging gate at 6.12 (9.94), used to stop motorized vehicles. After the barrier the trail is rocky and intermediate and you reach the second decision point at 6.51 (10.48). This time, the common sense intermediate trail is on the right, the big rocks on the left. The two trails rejoin about 500 ft later. The trail continues rocky intermediate to the final decision point at 6.71 (10.79), this time easier to left, rocky expert to right. Again the two rejoin after about 500 ft.

After your last drop, the trail continues intermediate and fun. At 7.01 (11.28) there is a bridge across a small creek, followed by a barrier, and Creek Road at 7.06 mi (11.36 km). For the described ride this is the end of the trail section, at an elevation of about 920 ft (280 m) or a drop of 360 ft (110 m) from the trailhead.

Turn right and ride along Creek Rd, reaching route 30 at 9.39 (15.11). Turn right (north) and continue. At 13.70 (22.05) turn right and climb Pumpkin Hollow Rd back to the starting trailhead, reached at 15.35 mi (24.70 km).

9

Irishtown-Minerva Stream Trail

Expert

Distance: 15.1 mi (24.3 km), 11.5 mi off-road plus 3.6 mi on roads

Difficulty: Expert, except easy intermediate first 2.5 mi to Boreas River

Climbing Required: 200 ft on road at end, 800 ft drop on off-road section

Time to ride: 3.5 to 6 hours

Wild Forest: Vanderwhacker Mountain

General

This trail offers a wonderful ride with a lot of rocks, stream crossings and some wet areas. Excellent fitness and solid riding skills are needed. The off-road portion of the trail descends almost continuously. The trail crosses the Boreas River at a location where the old snowmobile bridge is probably washed out, so crossing may be difficult in high water. The trail may be wet in the spring; the best riding is usually late summer and fall. A car shuttle is used for this ride.

Trail Access

To avoid an additional 20 mi of road riding, a car shuttle is required. Minerva Lake is a reasonable place to leave a car. From the Northway (I87) take Exit 26 (Pottersville) and Highway 19 to Olmstedville. Then the AP Morse Memorial road toward Minerva and Highway 28N. 0.5 mi before 28N, turn right on Long Hill Road, drive 0.1 mi and turn left into Minerva Lake and leave a car(s). From Minerva Lake, return to the AP Morse Memorial Highway, turn right and drive .5 mi west to Highway 28N. Turn right (northwest) on 28N and drive 14.3 mi to Highway 2. Turn right again and drive 5.6 mi east on Highway

2 (Blue Ridge Road) to the trailhead, which is on the right. The trailhead elevation is 1870 ft (570 m) and the coordinates are 581275, 4865565.

Description

Start riding south on the trail going downhill. At 0.30 mi (.48 km) there is a trail to the right; take this right turn. (The straight ahead trail ends at Cheney Pond) After the turn the trail is a soft grassy road about 8 ft wide, rated beginner or easy intermediate. The Boreas River/Lester Flow is reached at 2.5 (4.02).

The old road stops abruptly at the Boreas River. Wade across the river, or walk across the brush dam if it is there. Then hike about 150 ft south through the woods to find the trail. If you come to the trail where it is going both directions, go to the right. The intermediate rated trail on this side of the river is narrower, with a soft surface and some rocks. There may be some wet spots which have to be walked. A small stream is crossed at 3.0 (4.83). Around 4.0 (6.44) the trail becomes drier, downhill, rocky and expert rated. Another stream (it may be Minerva Stream, it is hard to tell on the USGS maps) is crossed at 4.8 (7.72). At 5.5 (8.85) there is a big wet spot that probably has to

Riders fearlessly cross the Boreas River.

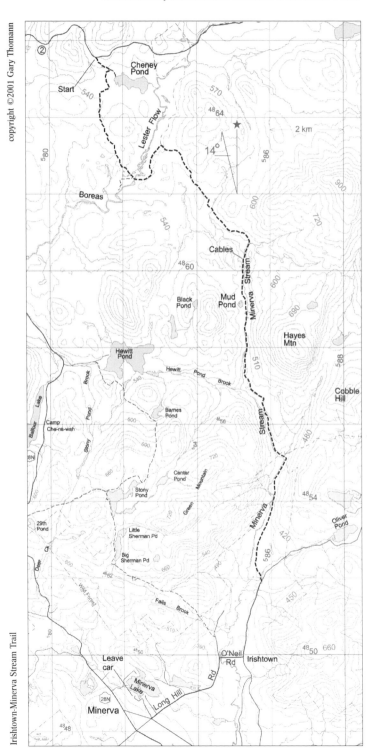

be walked. At 5.9 (9.49) the trail crosses another small stream, and then at 6.2 (9.98) crosses Minerva Stream at a point where a couple of cables are strung across. The trail continues rocky and expert. There may be wet spots, according to the season and recent rainfall. Mud Pond is passed at 6.8 (10.94). There are some buildings at 7.0 (11.26), and then the trail turns into a washed out road, which has been eroded to bedrock, still rated advanced. The road descends slightly, which assists in keeping the bike upright and in motion. At 7.3 (11.75), Minerva stream is crossed again.

Around 9.8 (15.77), the eroded road gradually becomes less technical, eventually becoming Byrnes Road. County Highway 24 (Irish Town Road/Hoffman Road) is reached at 11.5 (18.50). Turn south on Highway 24, then at 13.1 (21.08) turn right (west) on O'Neil Road and ride to Long Hill Road, reached at 13.5 (21.72). Turn left and ride (and climb) south to Minerva Lake at 15.1 mi (24.30 km). If it is warm, a dip in the lake will be inviting.

10

Knapp Estate Hogtown Loop
Expert

Distance: 9.53 mi (15.34 km) in and out

Difficulty: Expert

Climbing: 2070 ft (630 m)

Time to ride: 3 to 5 hours

Wild Forest: Lake George (east side)

General

This is arguably the best ride in the Adirondacks for skilled riders. It has everything; big drops, brutal climbs, superb singletrack and great views. And after the ride you can swim in the lake. The ride takes place on the old Knapp estate, purchased in 1894 on the spur of the moment by George O. Knapp, cofounder of the Union Carbide Corporation. Well managed as a wild area by Mr. Knapp, most of the estate was sold to New York State in 1941. There are a lot of trails on the estate you can ride, several can be seen on the ride map. Because of the elevation changes, they are all pretty challenging. Close to the Hogtown parking area begins a trail up Buck Mountain. Whether posted or not, I believe this trail is closed to riding.

Trail Access

To get to the Hogtown trailhead; leave the Northway (I87) at Exit 20, drive north on Highway 9 for a few hundred feet and turn east on Highway 149. Set your trip odometer to 0.0 as you turn east. At 3.1 mi cross Bay road at a stoplight and continue east. At 4.6 mi cross 9L at a stoplight, continuing east on 149. At this 149/9L junction there is a Stewarts, the last place to get supplies/gas if needed. At 6.1 mi turn left (north) on Buttermilk Road; in 2000 there was a Black Rooster Stoves shop at this point. At 9.3 mi Tyler Wood road comes in from the right; continue on north. About 9.6 mi the pavement will end, and somewhere along here the road name changes to Sly Pond road. At 12.65 mi there is a small trailhead on the left, with a trail that goes over to the Village of Pilot Knob; just continue driving north. At 15.1 mi a road goes off to the right; continue north on what is now Shelving Rock road, and at 15.9 mi pull into the Hogtown trailhead parking lot on the right. The parking lot elevation is 1300 ft (396 m) and the coordinates are 615855, 4820585.

Description

There are a couple of options on this ride; I will explain the basic ride and then discuss the options. From the north end of the parking lot start riding on the old road. At .59 mi (.95 km) there is a turn off to the left, with a barrier a little ways down the trail; this trail to the left is sometimes called the Old Farm Road. Skip it and continue riding north on the road to Dacy Clearing. At .96 (1.54) and 1.12 (1.80) you will cross small streams. At 1.29 (2.07) there is a clearing with some old foundations; all that is left of some of the Jack Dacy farm buildings. Turn left on the trail going west and after a couple hundred feet, go around a vehicle barrier. Just beyond the barrier there is sign with distances to Shelving Rock Road/Mtn of 2.4 and 3.7 mi, respectively.

You're now riding the Shortway trail, continue west, descending as you go. At 1.52 (2.44) a stream flows across, and then the trail gets a little more difficult and fun, intermediate maybe. At 1.60 (2.58) there is a bridge, and at 1.78 (2.86) the Old Farm Road comes in from the left. There is also a trail going off to the right (north). Continue descending east on Shortway, where you will encounter some nice rocky sections and, if you raise your head, see a stream on the right. At 2.41 (3.88) a bridge is crossed and at 2.58 (4.15) a bridge crosses a larger stream. At this point you have experienced 560 ft (170 m) of elevation drop fun.

At 2.65 (4.26) there is a junction and some more signs. The trail to the left is, I believe, named Big Bridges. But, for this ride continue east on Shortway, following the sign for Shelving Rock Road/Mtn. At 2.83 (4.56) a bridge crosses Shelving Rock Brook, and at 3.02 (4.86) there is junction with a trail to the right (north); make the right turn and about a hundred feet up the trail are several signs. In the direction you will be riding (north) a signboard states Erebus Mtn - 2.6 mi along with distances to other places. A sign indicates there is a trail going west, but it may be hard to see; this westward trail is overgrown and should probably be abandoned.

At any rate, for this ride continue north; you are now about to pay for your lazy descent, with a climb of 540 ft (165 m) in the next 1.21 mi (1.94 km) on an intermediate trail. All sections of the ascent are rideable, but I expect most of you will not be able to climb it without a dab or two. At 3.56 (5.72) a trail to the right climbs back up to Dacy Clearing. This trail to the right is the Longway trail, and in my experience is usually muddy and less fun than Shortway. Continue riding onward, upward and northward on the Erebus

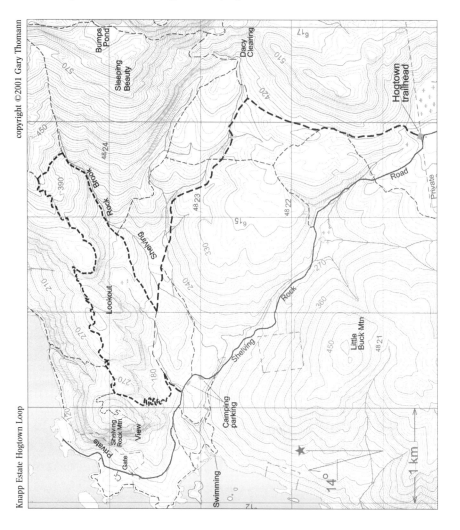

trail; at 3.66 (5.89) a bridge crosses a small creek which flows into Shelving Rock Brook, now running alongside the trail. At 4.23 (6.80), after a particularly tough little rise, you reach the end of this climb at a junction. The trail going north continues to climb, but for this ride turn left (west again); one of the signs at the junction states that the left turn takes you to the Lakeshore in 2.1 mi, a vista at 0.9 mi and Shelving Rock Mtn at 3.0 mi. You will see the mountain and a vista on this ride, but hopefully won't arrive at the Lakeshore.

The trail to the west climbs steeply, and you will have to push your bike on

The view is worth the pain of the uphill ride to Shelving Rock Mountain.

part of it; it is a difficult trail section to ride even descending when riding in the opposite direction. At about 4.47 (7.20) you climb to a T, and more signs. Go left and start riding south; a sign will again mention the lakeshore, vista and Shelving Rock Mtn. After starting south, the trail will turn to the right and climb to the top of a knoll. Here you are privileged to enter the chocolate cheese cake of mountain bike trails, sweet and challenging singletrack! I won't attempt a detailed description, just expect rocks, sharp turns, some short but very steep descents, switchbacks, two foot drop offs and some wet spots. If it has rained recently and the trail surface is wet, it may even be more fun than you can handle. I will just mention the important landmarks. At 4.90 (7.89) there is a trail to the right (west) with a sign for the lakeshore and a vista. Don't take this trail, continue going south. At 5.34 (8.60) you come to a rock ledge with a beautiful view to the south; stop here, rest for a minute, and enjoy again the trail you just rode.

After the vista, the trail turns to the north for a while, and then continues its wicked ways, swinging west, south, west, south... At 6.69 (10.77), after crashing down a series of sharp switchbacks, there is a trail junction, with trails going both south and north. There are several trail signs here. Go south, the sign states Shelving Rock mtn/road as .9 and 1.4 mi respectively. At 6.97 (11.22) you tumble out on a road, having eaten and hopefully digested your singletrack cheesecake, although the fun is not yet over. For the described ride, I will assume a left turn at this point to go back east. However, if you have the energy, go to the right and climb to the top of Shelving Rock Mountain and enjoy the view of Lake George. The Sagamore Hotel is visible across the lake, and just below on the east shore you can see the private land and buildings which remain of the Knapp estate, now owned by his heirs.

Turn left and start down the old carriage road; although wide, it is much eroded and very challenging in spots. The descent involves a long series of neat switchbacks. At 7.86 (12.64) there is a junction, with a trail going left and right. If you go left, you can climb back up on the Shortway trail, a very difficult climb. Having some mercy, I suggest you turn right and go south to the Shelving Rock trailhead on Shelving Rock Road, reached at 8.02 (12.90). Now you can turn left (east) and climb 900 ft (276 m) back to the cars, reached at 9.53 (15.34). After what you have been through, even a road climb may be challenging, but hopefully you will have a demented grin on your face when you reach the parking lot.

As mentioned before, there are optional ways to do this ride. One way is to not turn into the Hogtown parking area, but to drive on down Shelving Rock Road and park. The big climb at the end of the ride is avoided (however, the initial descent down the Shortway trail is lost). The lower down parking areas are marked on the map. The first two big areas are for nearby camping, and on weekends may be close to full and boisterous. You may want to park a little lower down at the lots where camping is not allowed. From any of these parking lots you can ride over to the Shelving Rock trailhead and work your way up to where the Erebus trail goes north from the Shortway trail, which gets you into the loop, so to speak. Another option, if you have more than one car, is a shuttle to place a car(s) in one of the lower lots, while still leaving from the Hogtown trailhead. At the end, this car will be available to take tired riders back to the top. However you do the ride, if it is a warm day ride your bike to the swimming spot marked on the map and relax for a while. If you want to learn more about the old Knapp estate, get a copy of Sweet Peas and a White Bridge by Elsa Kny Steinbeck (the Crandall library in Glens Falls has a copy); it has several excellent pictures of the old Knapp estate and Dacy farm.

northeast

There is not a large amount of Wild Forest acreage in the northeast part of the park because this region is dominated by the wilderness classified areas, High Peaks, McKenzie Mountain, Sentinel Range, Hurricane Mountain, Giant Mountain and Dix Mountain. However, riding can be found in the four areas that do exist, Hammond Pond, Saranac Lakes, Taylor Pond, Debar Mountain and the north edge of Vanderwhacker Mountain. These rides are easily reachable from the popular destination areas of Lake Placid and Saranac Lake. I have found seven rides for you in the northeast section, none rated more difficult than intermediate. If you want to find additional rides, go to the local bike stores listed at the end of this guide and ask the staff to tell you their favorites. There are also ski areas in the northeast where you can mountain bike. These ski areas are also listed at the end of the guide.

11

Old Road to Santanoni Preserve

Beginner

Distance: 9.0 mi (14.5 km) out and back

Difficulty: Beginner

Climbing Required: 400 ft (120 m)

Time to ride: 1.5 to 3 hours

Wild Forest: Vanderwhacker Mountain (north edge)

General

This ride is a wonderful afternoon cruise on an old gravel/dirt road through the woods, to Newcomb Lake. The surface is beginner, with an occasional sandy section which requires harder pedaling. There is a gentle but nearly continuous rise in elevation most of the way in, then a gentle 100 ft drop to the lake. On the return, after the initial climb, you can almost coast all the way back to the trailhead. The stone bridges on the road, and the old buildings of Camp Santanoni on the shore of the lake are scenic lagniappe.

Trail Access

The trail begins at the Santanoni Preserve headquarters northwest of Newcomb. From Highway 28N, 0.3 mi west of the Newcomb Town Hall (and 2.2 mi west of the road into the Harris Lake campground) turn north at the Santanoni Preserve sign. After turning north there is another immediate left turn. If you see a sign "Three Ton Bridge" you are doing okay. Drive 0.4 mi to the headquarters buildings; there is parking on the right. The parking lot elevation is 1595 ft (486 m) and the coordinates are 567025, 4868940.

Description

Ride north around the vehicle gate onto the 12 ft wide gravel/dirt road which begins a gentle climb. The surface is beginner, with an occasional sandy spot which is harder to pedal. At 0.9 mi (1.45 km) there are some buildings on both sides of the road, apparently old farm buildings. The road continues to climb gently, with an occasional section steep enough that standing on the pedals might be required. At 2.1 (3.38) ride over a bridge with rock railings along the side. At 2.2 (3.54) there is a junction. The road to the left to Moose Pond immediately enters the High Peaks Wilderness area. You cannot ride it. There is sign saying Wilderness Area. Take the right fork and continue the gentle climbing. The top of the climb is reached at 2.8 (4.51), it is level for a bit, and at 3.0 (4.83) a descent begins. At 3.3 (5.31) two more of the stone rail bridges are ridden across. At 3.6 (5.79) a trail with red markers goes off to the left (north). This trail goes around Newcomb Lake, but it immediately enters Wilderness classified land, so it also cannot be ridden; continue straight. At 3.9 (6.28) the road crosses a wooden bridge over a narrow part of Newcomb Lake/Upper Duck Hole, and then swings left alongside the eastern edge of the lake. At 4.5 mi (7.24 km) the road ends at the camp, several large buildings with

The old road into the Santanoni Preserve.

huge porches, a good place to sit and eat a snack. The trail on around the lake, mentioned earlier, also starts from the camp, but again it immediately goes into Wilderness. The ride back is on the same road. After climbing a short distance to the highest elevation, you can coast almost all the way back to the trailhead.

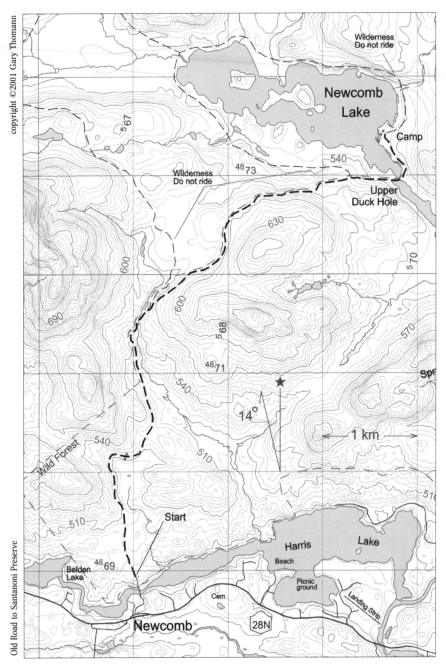

Watch your speed and the sandy spots; it is possible to crash anywhere, and you don't want to run into somebody hiking in.

12

Hays Brook Truck Trail
Beginner/Intermediate

Distance: 13.1 mi (21.1 km) for complete tour

Difficulty: Beginner with one section of intermediate singletrack

Climbing Required: 500 ft (150 m)

Time to ride: 2 to 3 hours

Wild Forest: Debar Mountain

General

This is a wandering ride on several old roads, generally beginner rated, with occasional climbs and descents and some roots in the road surface. There is a nice section of intermediate singletrack which can be left out if desired. An old meadow with a corral is one of the destinations, Hays Brook the other. This ride has several parts and is easily shortened.

Trail Access

From the intersection of NY 30 & 192 (at Paul Smiths), drive 3.8 mi north on NY 30, and turn right onto a hard surface road. Drive another 1/4 mi and park in a lot on left just as road begins to curve around to the right. The elevation here is 1595 ft (486 m) and the coordinates are 557165, 4925350.

Description

From the parking lot, there is a truck trail heading off straight north. Don't take this old road; it only goes two tenths of a mile and then ends. Instead, follow the blacktop road on around. At less than 0.1 mi (.16 km) there is a trail to the left; bypass this trail and continue on the road a couple hundred feet to a second trail with a gate across it. Ride around the gate and start north. At 0.3 (.48) you will see the first trail joining from the left. Ride over the Osgood River on a sturdy bridge at 0.5 (.80). Just a few hundred feet past the bridge, there is a singletrack trail to the left and about 50 ft further a road to the right (the Grass Pond trail). These trails will be ridden later; for now continue straight on the road up a pretty sharp climb. At 1.3 (2.09) there is a Y junction. The road to the left will be ridden later; stay to the right and continue on the road, riding slightly east of north.

There is a downhill section at about 1.6 (2.57), and the road bends around to the east. A clearing is reached at 2.7 (4.34), and the trail turns to the north and narrows. Ride on north until you reach Hays Brook. You can cross the brook and continue, but I believe the trail ends shortly. For the assigned ride, turn around and ride back to the Y intersection, reached at about 4.2 (6.76). This time, take what would have been the left turn and ride west.

The beginner rated road begins with a long downhill and curves around to the north. At 4.7 (7.56) there is a trail to the left which you may not notice; in any case continue straight on the road. There is a bridge over Hays Brook at 4.9 (7.88) with a steep climb just after the bridge. After this climb, the old road has occasional descents and ascents, and some roots in the road. The road ends at the old sheep meadow containing two leantos and a small stable at 6.7 (10.78). Just before the road ends there is a narrower trail off to the left (north), which you can explore if desired. But, for the described ride, turn around and start riding back on the road.

Coming back on the old road, about two-tenths of a mile after recrossing Hays Brook, there is a singletrack to the right at 8.7 (14.0). This trail is very narrow with some nice climbs and descents, rated intermediate. You can either turn right and ride this trail, or skip it and continue to return on the road. For this description, it will be ridden; turn right and go. At 9.6 (15.45) this singletrack ends on the road just north of the Osgood River, where you were earlier. Go north on the road about 50 ft and then turn east (right) on the Grass Pond trail, which is again a beginner rated road, with some climbs and drops. A stream is crossed at 10.5 (16.89). A clearing is reached beside Grass

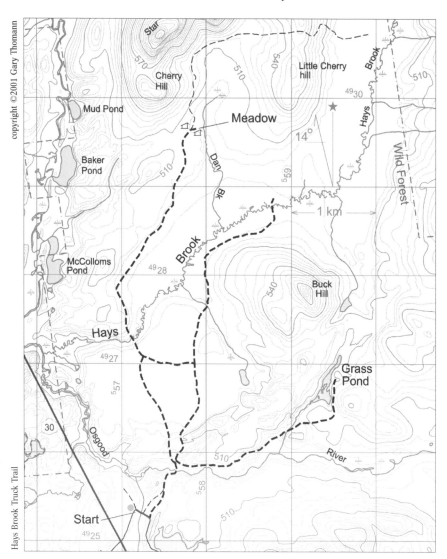

Pond at 10.8 mi, and the road turns left. You may continue riding, but for the described ride turn around, ride back out to the first road, south over the Osgood River, through the woods past Grandma's place and back to the car at 13.1 mi (21.08).

13

Floodwood Loop
Beginner/Intermediate

Distance: 9.2 mi (14.8 km) for the loop

Difficulty: Beginner/intermediate

Climbing Required: 200 ft (60 m)

Time to ride: 2 to 3 hours

Wild Forest: Saranac Lakes

General

On this loop you get to wander through the many ponds and small lakes around the Fish Creek Campground, on a trail about 3 ft wide, with few rocks but quite a few bumpy roots. Although the topography here is not mountainous, you still get some ascents and descents. Unlike the 30 m contours of the other maps, the one for this ride has 15 m main contours.

Trail Access

The ride begins from the Fish Creek public campground. From the intersection of Highways 3 and 30 east of Tupper Lake, drive north 5.5 mi on Highway 30 and then turn left (west) into the campground. The trailhead is 0.3 mi into the campground, across from campsite 23. A signboard states Fish Creek Loop, along with some distances for various destinations. The trailhead elevation is 1575 ft (480 m) and the coordinates are 551000, 4905960.

Description

Start north on a narrow hard surfaced road. At a distance slightly greater than 0.1 mi (.16 km) turn right just in front of the building containing bath facilities (going straight would be riding the loop in the other direction.) The trail narrows to 3 ft wide, with a dirt surface. On much of the ride there will be roots in the trail. There will also be an occasional wet spot. There is a sharp left at 0.6 (.97). At 1.0 (1.61) a trail crosses; continue straight.

At 1.4 (2.25) Horsehoe Pond is on the right. The trail then goes part way into the "shoe," abruptly swings west, and then at 2.1 (3.38) turns right to go north again. Horseshoe Pond remains on the right as you ride north. The northwest edge of the pond is reached at 2.6 (4.18), at a drop down to a snowmobile bridge at the pond outflow. There is likely to be a wet spot in front of the bridge that has to be walked. The trail continues about 3 ft wide, with the roots providing bumps.

At 3.5 (5.63) there is a log bridge with the logs running in the same direction as the trail; it has to be walked. There is a T junction at 3.8 (6.11); turn left. (The right turn goes to a part of Polliwog Pond). At 4.0 (6.44) there is another junction; turn right and Floodwood Road is reached at 4.2 (6.76). There is a sign stating Snowmobile Trail at this trailhead. Turn left (west) and ride the road for a mile.

At 5.2 (8.37) a second trailhead is reached; there are no signs, just some snowmobile disks on the trees. Turn left (south) off the road and start riding this trail. The trail begins about 7 ft wide and very easy, but soon goes back to a character similar to what was ridden earlier. There is a sharp drop and a snowmobile bridge at 5.4 (8.69). At 5.7 (9.17) there is a T; turn right (west). (The left fork goes to Middle Pond). At 5.8 mi there is a trail fork; take the left fork.

The trail continues bumpy with lots of roots. At 5.9 (9.49) a bridge across a small stream has to be walked, because the logs are again laid in the riding direction. There is a sharp climb right after the bridge, and Floodwood Pond will show up on the right. At 6.4 (10.3) there will probably be a wet boggy area that has to be walked. Then there is another of those bridges that has to be walked, and then another sharp climb. At 6.7 (10.78) there is a campsite with a picnic table and a canoe launch. This is a good place for rest and a snack.

Continuing south a few hundred feet from the campsite there is a fork; take the trail to the left. The trail now has fewer roots for a while, and generally drops. The riding is very easy. At about 7.2 (11.58) campsites appear along the trail. At 7.7 (12.39) the roots begin again, and then the trail becomes very bumpy, with even more roots than earlier. At 9.1 (14.64) the building with the bathroom facilities is reached again. Ride south back down the hard surfaced lane to the trailhead at 9.2 mi 14.80 km).

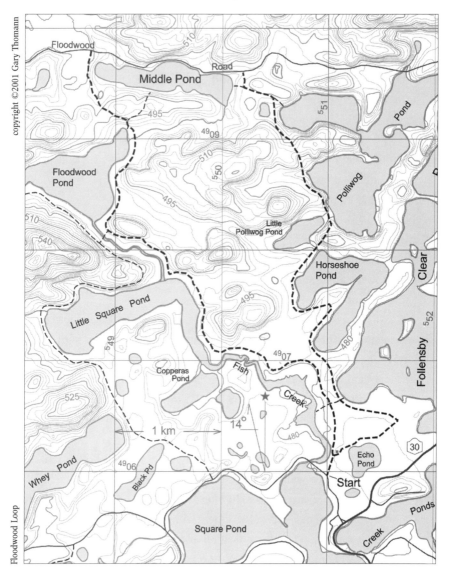

Floodwood Loop

14

Distance: 9.5 mi (15.3 km) for the complete loop

Difficulty: Intermediate with a beginner section

Climbing Required: 400 ft (120 m)

Time to ride: 2 to 3 hours

Wild Forest: Saranac Lakes

General

This ride takes you to a beautiful view overlooking Deer Pond, on a loop composed of three distinctly different types of trail - one section of singletrack, one section about 4 ft wide which allows a little more maneuvering, and a section of old blacktop road and grassy road that is beginner. The singletrack and 4 ft section offer splendid riding for intermediate rated riders.

Trail Access

The ride will be described from Bull Point trailhead, although the loop also touches Highway 30/3 in two other places. From the village of Saranac Lake, drive southwest about 11 mi on Highway 3, turn right (north) on Highway 45 and go 2.4 mi to Highway 30, at Wawbeek. Turn right (north) and go 0.7 mi further, the trailhead is on the left. There is parking at the trailhead for 5 or 6 cars. Or from Tupper Lake drive east 4.5 mi on Highway 3/30 and take 30 north when the two routes split; the trailhead will be 1.7 mi further on the left. From the north, at Saranac Inn, go south about 9.0 mi on Highway 30 and the trailhead will be on the right. The elevation at the trailhead is 1625 ft (495 m) and the position is 551945, 4900875.

Description

At the trailhead is a signboard stating it is 2.4 mi to Deer Pond and 6.6 miles to Route 3 via Deer Pond Loop. Ride west on the old soft road through the woods, level and beginner rated. At 0.6 mi (.97 km) a small wooden bridge is crossed and at 0.7 (1.13) there is a junction; signboards state it is 0.7 mi back to Route 30 at Bull Point, to the left 1.2 mi to the Route 3 Parking Area, to the right 1.7 mi to Deer Pond and 3.6 mi to Old Wawbeek Road. Take the right fork.

After the right turn, the trail is singletrack, not technically difficult, but intermediate rated because it is so narrow. At 0.9 (1.45) there is a 200 ft long bog (stringer) bridge, built from split logs with the flat side up, parallel to the trail. There are two logs laid side by side, with about two inches of space between them. You probably want to walk this bridge; it is extremely difficult to ride because if the front wheel drifts even slightly off line, it will either fall off the side or into the crack between the two logs.

Just after the bog bridge, at 1.1 (1.77), there is some old corduroy which is rideable. The trail continues as singletrack a foot or two wide, but not technically difficult. At 1.3 (2.09) there is another of those bog bridges with about a one foot drop off at each end; it is best to walk across it. At 1.5 (2.41) there will probably be a wet spot. At 1.7 (2.74) there is a short sharp rideable climb. At 1.9 (3.06) there is another bridge, and then a short sharp climb with some rocks on the bottom part, which may be rideable for a very good climber. The trail continues very narrow. Just after the hill, there is a small stream crossing that is rocky and tricky, and then at 2.2 mi there is another sharp climb that is difficult to ride. Then the trail starts to drop and at 2.5 (4.02) reaches a trail junction, with a signboard giving various distances. Take the right turn to visit Deer Pond; immediately there is a sharp drop on the singletrack with a rideable bridge at the bottom. At 2.6 (4.18) Deer Pond is reached. Walk down to the shore, rest awhile and have a snack; the scenery is beautiful.

From Deer Pond it is possible to ride further north. However, for the described loop, ride back south to the trail junction at 2.7 (4.34) and turn right (south). A signboard indicates it is 1.9 mi to Old Wawbeek Road. The trail begins with a drop followed by some intermediate rated riding. The south edge of Deer Pond is on the right, another nice view. This trail is about 4 ft wide, which is wider than the singletrack into Deer Pond, so there is a little more room to maneuver. At 2.9 (4.67) there is a drop and then another of those

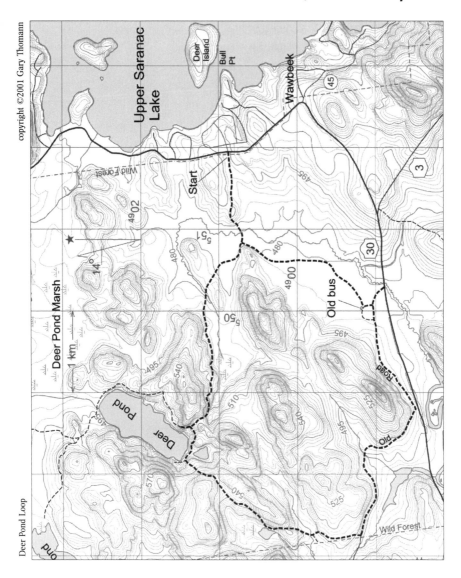

bridges, although this one is easier to ride because the planks are wider. Right after the bridge there is a short climb; if you ride the drop and the bridge fast enough you can reach the top of the climb. Right after this climb, there is a trail going off to the right which goes down to the west side of Deer Pond; for the described ride continue south on the main trail, which leaves the pond. Almost immediately there is a hard climb, which is not technically difficult but requires considerable fitness.

The trail continues to climb until 3.2 (5.15), and then begins to descend. The trail remains about 4 ft wide, with rocks in the trail which require maneuvering to avoid; a wonderful trail for riding. At 3.8 (6.11) there is a little pond on the right. The trail descends right to the edge of the pond, and for one or two hundred feet there is a very difficult rocky wet section. All except advanced riders will want to walk this short section.

Right after the pond there is a climb about 200 feet long that requires some fitness. The top is reached at 4.0 (6.44), and a fast descent begins; look well ahead of the bike for roots and rocks. At 4.2 (6.76) the trail crosses a bridge over a small stream; here the planks are crossways to the trail, so it is easy to ride. Right after the bridge there is a trail junction; stay to the left. The trail begins to climb again, reaching the top of the climb at 4.4 (7.08). Then the trail drops again, and becomes more technical, with lots of roots in the trail which makes riding the trail resemble descending stairs. At the bottom of the descent, Old Wawbeek Road is reached at 4.7 (7.56)

The rest of the ride is beginner rated. Turn left (east) on Old Wawbeek Road, an ancient hard surfaced road grown over enough that it is only about 8 ft wide. At 6.0 (9.65), the trail momentarily touches Highway 3/30, and this is another location where the loop could be started. Continue riding east on the old road.

At 6.7 (10.78) there is a road going off to the left (north). This is the west end of a horseshoe loop. Continue straight and at 6.9 (11.10) the other end of the loop is seen. To see another trailhead, continue east on the hard pavement and Highway 3/30 is reached again at 7.1 (11.42). For the described ride, turn around and ride back to east end of the horseshoe and turn right into the horseshoe. Ride a few hundred feet to an old iron bar on the right across a trail, trip distance 7.4 (11.91). (If you come to an old bus, you have gone too far; the iron bar and trail is behind you.) Turn right, go around the bar and head north.

The trail north is an old grassy road through the woods, beginner rated with an occasional root in it. At 8.7 (14.0), the first trail junction is again reached. Turn right (east) and ride back to the parking lot at Bull Point, reached at 9.5 mi (15.29 km).

15

Meacham Lake to Debar Meadow
Intermediate

Distance: 18.4 mi (29.7 km) out and back

Difficulty: Intermediate

Climbing Required: 800 ft (244 m)

Time to ride: 3 to 6 hours

Wild Forest: Debar Mountain

General

A nice long ride on 6 - 10 ft wide roads, with a grassy/leafy/pine needle surface. Some sections are rutted, and others have combinations of corduroy, rocks and roots. There are lots of wet areas, so best to ride during reasonably dry conditions (not a good spring ride). This trail would benefit greatly from some drainage and bridge work. A beginning rider could attempt this ride, and the ride can be shortened simply by turning around earlier.

Trail Access

From the intersection of NY 30 & 192 at Paul Smiths, drive north on NY 30. The southern entrance to the Meacham Lake campground appears at 9.9 mi, but we will use the northern one. Continue north on 30 to 12.3 mi and turn right at a small Meacham Lake sign. After the turn, continue to 12.8 mi and turn left into the campground; the entrance booth is reached at 13.1 mi. After the entrance booth continue straight east to 13.3 mi, turn left on CS42 and go north to where the road leaves the camping loop at 13.4 mi (you will be across from campsite 36). There will be a sign for Debar Mountain Trail. Continue driving to 13.8 mi to the gravel pit parking lot. Elevation at the parking lot is 1595 ft (486 m), coordinates are 557600, 4936620.

Description

The trail begins at the sign-in box and gate at the east end of the gravel pit parking lot. Start riding on the wide beginner road. At 0.84 mi (1.35 km) there is a double track going off to the left; continue straight. Immediately afterward a small stream is crossed. At 0.98 (1.58) the Debar Mountain trail goes off to the left; for this ride take the trail to the right toward Debar Meadows (distance listed as 5.0 mi on the sign, but actually 6.5). You will now occasionally see yellow horse trail and orange snowmobile trail markers along the route.

At 1.15 (1.85), a small stream, flowing south, is crossed, and the outflow at the southern edge of Winnebago Pond is crossed at 1.42 (2.28). The trail begins to climb and becomes intermediate rated, with corduroy, rocks and perhaps wet areas. There is a wooden bridge over a small creek at 2.02 (3.25). In this area there are about 30 tree stumps and some rocks. You may notice an old spur trail which goes to the right around the stumps/rocks; apparently once a detour for horses.

The highest elevation on the ride is reached around 2.3 (3.70) at 1800 ft (550 m), 200 ft above the start. At 2.55 (4.10) a metal culvert is crossed and at 2.62 (4.22) another small stream is crossed. There may be some large wet areas in this trail section Another metal culvert is crossed at 2.91 (4.68) and then a 10 ft stream, flowing south, is crossed at 3.25 (5.23). There may be a damaged wooden bridge across this creek. The stream crossing elevation is 1700 ft (518 m).

Another stream appears at 3.42 (5.50). You will probably have to walk across it. The ruins of a bridge may be visible. There is an uphill section and then a downhill to 4.21 (6.77), where there is a large blue circle on a tree, and a trail going off to the right. For this ride, continue east (left or straight, according to how the trail junction is interpreted). A couple of culverts are crossed at 4.5 (7.24). At 5.46 mi there is a four post barrier and then the trail hits a better road. For the described ride continue straight ahead on this road. The trail enters a marshy section at 5.98 (9.62). If you are lucky, there will be a beaver dam along the left side of the road, 3 ft high and 300 ft long, keeping the road dry.

At 6.06 (9.75) there is a double track and a small pond to the right;

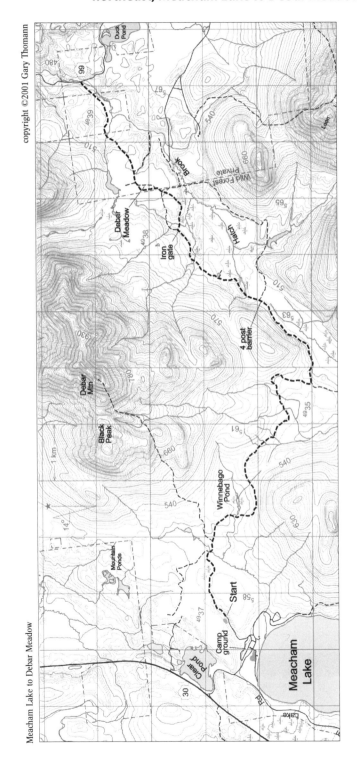

Meacham Lake to Debar Meadow

continue straight on the main trail. A small stream is crossed on a culvert at 6.42 (10.33), and an iron gate is passed at 6.81 (10.96). Just beyond the gate there is a spur trail to the left; for this ride stay right. At 7.43 there is a trail crossing. The trail from the left is the spur trail coming back in; the road to the right goes south about 0.5 mi to Hatch Brook. For the described ride stay straight on the main trail into Debar Meadow. The trail enters private land for about the next mile. The trail splits briefly, you can go either left or right. There are several old building foundations in the meadow. At 7.75 (12.47), at the northeast edge of the meadow, there is an old road to the left and also a cross-bar from which a sign probably once hung. For the described ride, continue straight (east).

At 7.92 (12.74) a T intersection is reached. To the right the road has a gate across it; go left (actually more like straight ahead since the intersection is at a curve in the road). The trail goes through another public wild forest section, and then at 9.18 (14.77), Highway 99 is reached just a few feet north of a concrete bridge across Hatch Brook. The elevation here is 1600 ft (488 m), about the same as the start at the gravel pit. Turn around and re-ride the trail back to the starting point.

16

Pine Pond
Intermediate

Distance: 14.4 mi (23.2 km) in and out

Difficulty: Intermediate

Climbing Required: 1000 ft (300 m)

Time to ride: 2 to 4 hours

Wild Forest: Saranac Lakes

General

This ride is on an old road through the woods to Pine Pond and Oseetah Lake, southwest of Lake Placid. It is easy intermediate, except in the first 1.1 mi there is an intermediate rated climb and descent. Apparently, this trail is always wet, and virtually impassable in the spring, so ride this trail when it has been dry. Even so, be prepared to get muddy. According to APA officials, the road is the boundary between the Saranac Lakes wild forest on the north and the High Peaks wilderness area to the south. However, the 1999 official APA land classification map has the boundary placed differently, making it appear that the old road dips into the wilderness zone. I have included the boundary as shown on the APA map, but remember that it is okay to ride the road, just don't take any offshoot trails going south because you will immediately go into the High Peaks Wilderness.

Trail Access

From Highway 73 just south of Lake Placid (just north of the Olympic ski jumps and across from the horse show grounds), turn northwest on Old

Military Road. Drive/ride 1.7 mi and then turn left on Averyville Road. At the turn, there will be a signboard for the Northville Placid Trail. Or, west of Lake Placid on highway 86 about 3.0 mi east of Ray Brook, go southeast on Old Military Road for 2.0 mi and make a right turn. Set your odometer at zero at the turn.

At 2.9 mi after the turn onto Averyville Road there is a fork; a dirt road continues straight ahead and the paved road swings to the right. Take the right fork and stay on the pavement. At 3.6 mi there is a dead-end sign; continue on and seemingly slide right through a farmyard onto what will now be a dirt road. At 4.1 mi there is a fork, with a sign stating that hikers and bikers should go left. Take the left fork, and immediately there will be a little opening with parking on the right side of the road. Elevation at this point is 2050 ft (625 m), and the coordinates are 575050, 4899050.

Description

Ride south on an old road about 12 ft wide with a dirt surface and some rocks. At 0.1 mi (.16 km) there is another small parking area on the right, and then the road turns to the west and starts to climb. The climb is intermediate rated; there are a lot of rocks in the road and some steep sections, but all is rideable. The top of the climb is reached at 0.4 (.64); at elevation 2205 ft (672 m). At the top there is only a short level section before the road begins descending, with some fairly steep intermediate rocky sections. There may be some muddy spots on the descent. The end of the steepest descent is reached at 1.1 (1.77), where there will probably be two big mud puddles.

The road becomes less rocky and descends gently, rated easy intermediate. Occasional wet spots will be encountered. At 1.4 (2.25) there is a fork. The fork to the left enters the wilderness area; it cannot be ridden. This is apparently an old access to the Northville Placid trail. Stay to the right. At 3.1 (5.0) there is a trail going off to the right (north). This trail goes in about a hundred feet to a camp; continue straight down the main trail. At 3.2 (5.15) there may be series of mud puddles. After the puddles the trail continues a gentle descent, staying easy intermediate. At 4.2 (6.76) there is a short sharp drop followed by a similar climb. At 4.3 (6.92) there is a little longer drop, with more roots in the trail.

At 4.5 (7.24) there is a fork; take the route to the right. At 4.7 (7.56) the road becomes a little narrower for a while and at 4.8 (7.72) there will probably be a

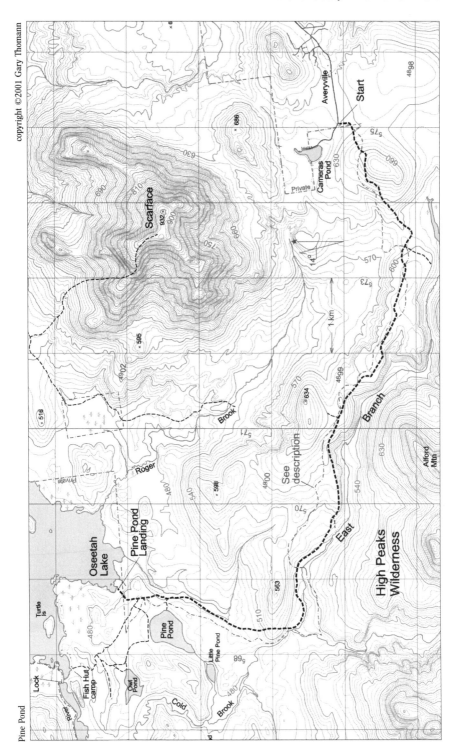

Pine Pond

long wet section. The trail continues to drop and is a little narrower than at the start, with fewer rocks but more roots. The East Branch of Cold Brook comes in from the left at 5.3 (8.53). Actually, the stream runs along south of the road for quite a distance, but it is only here that it is close enough to see. At 5.6 (9.0) the stream is still alongside, and there is a short climb that is rideable. After the climb the trail leaves the stream. The trail generally continues to descend, except for one or two short climbs. Pine Pond appears on the left at 6.7 (10.78) and there is a trail going down to the pond. Continue straight ahead. At 6.9 (11.10) there is another hard to see trail coming in from the left. Again, continue straight. At 7.0 (11.26), there is yet another trail coming in from the left. For now, also ignore this trail and continue straight. There is now a fairly steep drop, and at 7.2 (11.58) the trail comes to an end at Pine Pond Landing on the shore of Lake Oseetah. For the described ride you can return by the same route.

Making the uphill climb look easy, aren't they?

As can be seen from the map, private land begins just west of this last section of trail. I believe it is okay to go back up to the turn, and ride west down to Fish Hut camp across from the state locks. Respect any posted areas.

17

Moose Mountain Pond & Bass Lake
Intermediate

Distance: 12.2 mi (19.6 km) for the loop

Difficulty: Intermediate

Climbing Required: 655 ft (200 m)

Time to ride: 3 to 5 hours

Wild Forest: Hammond Pond

General

On this ride into Moose Mountain Pond leanto and back past Bass Lake you find great scenery on a true Adirondack trail, with lots of rocks and roots and sections of singletrack. In addition to the trail's numerous natural charms, a lot of rock work was done here several years ago by, I believe, inmates from the NY correctional system. Rock steps and a number of "paved" sections were installed, the pavement consisting of rocks laid in the trail with the flat side up. There are also a couple of log step sections. Just examining the trail work is worth the price of admission. The rock and log work was done with hikers in mind, and riding the constructed sections is both challenging and exciting.

Trail Access

Take exit 29 from the Northway (I87), set your trip odometer to zero, turn right and go 0.3 mi east to Highway 9. Turn left, go north, and at 2.8 mi turn right onto Essex county 4. Just a tenth of a mile after you turn, there is an old road on the right with an abandoned trailer on it; this is where you will ride out to the road later. For now continue driving, and 0.3 mi after the right turn angle right when the road forks; there will be a sign stating it is 13 mi to Port Henry, as well as some additional distances to other places. Continue until your odometer registers 5.8 mi and turn into the parking lot on the right; just a tenth of a mile or so after passing another small trailhead for the trail into Challis Pond. The elevation here is 950 ft (290 m) and the coordinates are 607275, 4871585.

Description

At the south edge of the parking lot there should be a sign which reads Berrymill Flow 1.4 mi, Bass Lake 2.4 mi, Moose Mountain Pond, 3.2 mi and Hammond Pond, 0.8 mi. Start riding south from the trailhead on a blue marked trail, easy for the first 0.3 mi (0.5 km), until a Y is encountered. The left fork of the Y (the original trail) goes down to the marsh and is probably not passable in all but the driest weather. For the described ride, take the right fork which climbs slightly to avoid the marsh. This section is technically much more difficult, singletrack with lots of roots and rocks, and the first of the rock work. After climbing up the ridge, the trail drops back down, and on the descent there are rock steps which are rideable, but certainly difficult, especially since you have only been riding for a few minutes.

At about 0.7 (1.1) you rejoin the original trail and continue south. At 1.0 (1.6) there is small waterfall on the left. Here the trail is generally easy except for a couple of tricky rock work sections. At 1.4 (2.3) you arrive at a trail junction; take the trail to the left to Moose Mountain Pond. About a tenth of a mile later you will cross Berrymill Brook on a wooden bridge, and then face some log steps which I don't think are rideable in this direction, although they can be ridden down on the return trip.

After the log steps, there is a 0.6 mi (1 km) section of challenging trail that is narrow, rocky and rooty. Included in this section is another set of log steps you have to walk up, and some neatly bench cut trail. After the challenging section the trail gets a little easier and is rideable all the way to Moose Mountain Pond except for a short but very steep climb and a couple of rocky sections. Just before getting to the leanto you will encounter the first of the rock pavement, in which rocks have been laid across a wet section. The rock path is only a foot or so wide, and the tops of the rocks don't quite align, so riding it is challenging!

When you reach the leanto at Moose Mountain Pond your bike computer

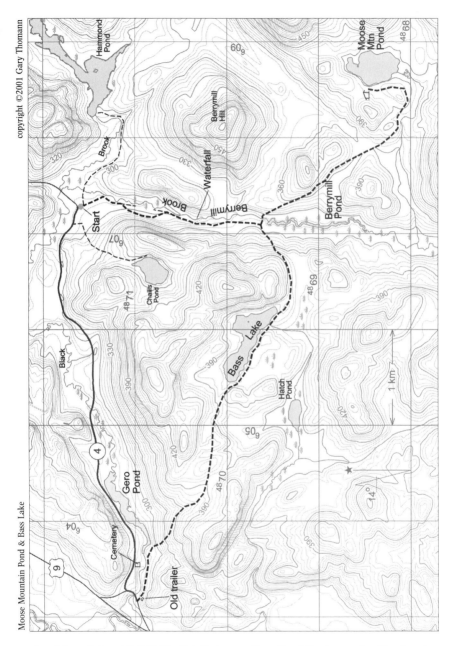

should read about 3.6 (5.8), slightly longer than the 3.2 mi promised by the sign at the trail head. The pond is a good place for a rest and food stop.

After the break, return to the trail junction by the same route you came in on. You will find the trail considerably easier and a lot of fun in this direction because you are gently descending. After riding down the log steps (if you wish to) and crossing Berrymill Brook on the wooden bridge you will come back to the trail junction at 5.8 (9.3). This time, take the other fork toward Bass Lake, heading southwest on a yellow marked trail.

Just after starting on this trail you will encounter a stringer bridge which is rideable, but very slick if wet. The trail is rideable for about three tenths of a mile, until you encounter some widely spaced rock steps that are probably not rideable upward. After the steps is a rocky section with a flat log placed in it. It can be ridden only by a very skilled rider. Following this section, there are a couple of long climbs that can be ridden.

The southeastern edge of Bass Lake is reached at 6.7 (10.8), where there is a rocky stretch that will have to be walked. Then the trail continues along the south edge of the lake. After crossing a little stream that is the lake outlet, the trail becomes much easier. It has a smooth dirt surface, with a couple of climbs and a stream crossing with rocks arranged on both sides so you can ride over the stream if you lift your front wheel across the 18 inch gap between the rocks. The easier trail continues all along the south side and around the western edge of the lake where the trail turns north.

Now there is an interesting section of small climbs and descents and five of those rock work sections, where you try to ride along the raised rock path.

Most of these also cross small streams so there are gaps in the path to get across. Each is probably rideable, but don't be disappointed if you don't manage to ride any; they are certainly tricky.

After the last of the five rock paths, you start a long downhill section which is fun and easy, except for a couple of rocky places. The trail comes down alongside Black Brook and then just a tenth of a mile or so further goes past the old trailer and ends at the road. Distance is about 9.2 (14.8) here. Turn right and ride the road back to the trailhead, which you should reach at 12.2 mi (19.6 km).

Think of the adventure you could be experiencing here.

southwest

The southwestern part of the park has a huge amount of public land, both Wilderness and Wild Forest. Silver Lake, West Canada Lake, Blue Ridge, Pigeon Lake and Ha-de-ron-dah are the wilderness areas, and the Wild Forests are Shaker Mountain, Ferris Lake, Black River, Moose River Plains, Sargent Ponds, Jessup River, Independence River, Fulton Chain and Blue Mountain.

In the winter, there is extensive snowmobile activity in the southwest Wild Forests. Old Forge and Inlet are popular winter destinations. In the summer, use is less intensive. If the existing trails could be well maintained, the southwest could support extensive mountain bike riding. However, keeping up with the maintenance is difficult, and it is not uncommon to encounter blowdown and areas needing drainage on the southwestern trails. I am describing here six rides which you should enjoy, one each in the first five areas listed above and a sixth on a town road.

18

Mitchell Ponds and Beaver Lake
Beginner

Distance: 12.2 mi (19.6 km), can be shortened or lengthened

Difficulty: Beginner

Climbing Required: Very little, approximately 200 ft (60 m)

Time to ride: 1.5 to 3 hours

Wild Forest: Moose River Plains/Moose River Recreation Area

General

This ride is consists of two scenic trails, each taking you into a small lake. The two trails are connected by a short stretch of the Moose River Recreation Area gravel road system. This is a relaxing beginner rated ride. It is a wonderful ride for a hot afternoon; you ride over the South Branch of the Moose River and can take a refreshing swim. The length of the ride can be increased by riding further on the gravel roads, or shortened by riding to only one of the ponds.

Trail Access

The ride begins at the Mitchell Ponds trailhead, reached by first turning south onto Limekiln road from NY 28 0.5 mi west of the village of Inlet. Drive south 1.9 mi to the ranger station, found on the left side of the road, where you register before continuing to the trailhead. (For a much longer ride, you can start riding here). To follow the prescribed ride, proceed through the entrance gate of the Moose River Recreation Area and drive 4.8 mi on the gravel road to a road fork, commonly known as the Rock Dam intersection. Bear left onto Moose River Road (not marked). The Red River is immediately crossed and then there is a second road fork. Take the right fork and drive 3.0 mi further to the Mitchell Ponds trailhead. Turn right onto the old two-track road and park in the grassy area 50 ft along the way. The elevation at the parking area is 1870 ft (570 m) and the coordinates are 523495, 4835885.

Description

The ride starts west on a smooth surfaced 8 ft wide dirt road. The road gradually climbs, although it may not be noticeable. At 1.8 mi (2.90 km) there is a trail off to the right (north) that is much narrower and is labeled as a snowmobile trail. It goes up to a difficult beaver dam crossing on a branch of the Red River and then proceeds to another Mitchell Ponds trailhead on Moose River Road 0.3 mi from the Rock Dam intersection. For this ride, ignore this side trail and continue straight ahead. At 1.9 (3.06) the east edge of Mitchell Lake is reached. The trail continues along the north edge of Mitchell Ponds, but is not included in this ride. Instead, ride back east to the trailhead. The road back out is fast, because the ponds are about 200 ft higher than the trailhead. As would be expected, Moose River Road is reached at 3.8 (6.11).

Turn right on the gravel road and ride south. There is an intersection at 4.2 mi; Moose River Road turns to the left. Instead, bear right onto Otter Brook Road. At 5.6 (9.01) the Beaver Lake trailhead is reached immediately after crossing the South Branch of the

A perfect day for a ride makes this rider very happy.

Moose River. Turn right (west) and ride west on a smooth road, slipping past a vehicle blocking gate at 5.8 (9.33). At 7.9 (12.71) the road changes to a path which drops rather steeply down to the shore of Beaver Lake. Scout this path and walk if it appears intimidating. The lake is reached at 8.0 (12.87). The return to the trailhead and Otter Brook Road is back on the same road, the

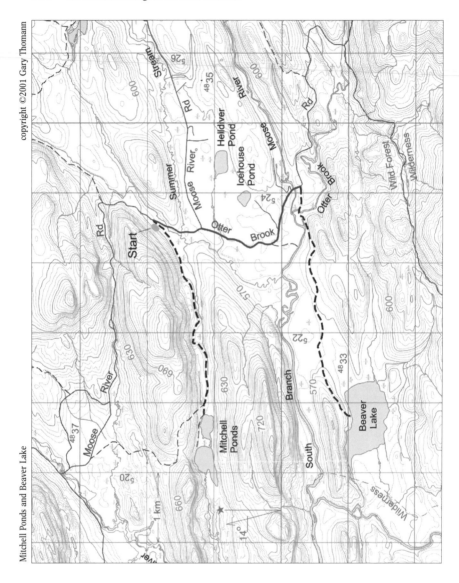

Mitchell Ponds and Beaver Lake

trailhead is again reached at 10.4 (16.73).

For the ride as assigned, ride north on the gravel roads to the cars, reached at 12.2 mi (19.63 km). There are other options. If it is hot, a swim in the river will feel great. The length of the ride can be increased by riding on the gravel roads in the recreational area.

19

Perkins Clearing
Beginner/Intermediate

Distance: 8.8 mi (14.2 km), out and back

Difficulty: Beginner, except of two intermediate rated climbs/descents

Climbing Required: 600 ft (180 m)

Time to ride: 2 to 3 hours

Wild Forest: Not Wild Forest, but a town road on IP land

General

This ride is different than the others in the guide. It is on a Town of Lake Pleasant road through land owned by the International Paper Company (IP), which is in turn largely surrounded by publicly owned land. In this area in the mid 80's there was a large land swap between IP and the state. The purpose of the swap was to consolidate the holdings of both parties; their interlocking ownership created a difficult to manage quilt. Although the swap was completed, it generated a lot of controversy, and from what I have read the final solution pleased nobody. The final terms of the swap created an orphan piece of Wild Forest classified land and some interesting regulations, which will be discussed in more detail later in this ride description.

The ride is on a dirt road. There are a few sections with corduroy across the road that are a little challenging for a beginner to ride, and on the way out there are two intermediate rated rocky climbs, each about 0.1 mi in length. These intermediate sections can be easily walked, so beginning riders should not be nervous about doing this ride. Besides the intermediate sections, there are several additional climbs and descents on the gravel roads. The land around the road has been logged recently, and there is a good chance of seeing wildlife.

An early morning ride on this road would probably be a scenic bonanza.

Trail Access

The described ride begins from Perkins Clearing. From the intersection of Highways 8 and 30 in the middle of Speculator, drive north 8.3 mi on 30 and turn left (south) on the dirt road at the north end of Mason Lake (it is possible to start riding at this point). Drive south 3.3 mi to Perkins Clearing, where there is a triangle about 0.1 mi on a side formed by three roads. Park somewhere around the triangle. The ride description starts at the eastern point of the road triangle.

Description

From the point of the road triangle, start riding east on the dirt road. At 0.2 mi (.32 km) there is a road off to the right, with an old camp on the left side of the road. IP has not given permission for public use of these side roads. For the described ride, continue straight.

The trail crosses the Jessup River on a bridge at a particularly scenic spot at 0.8 (1.29), and then at 0.9 (1.45) there is a road to the right. Continue straight. At 1.3 (2.09) there is a fork; take the road to the left. The road surface now becomes a little more challenging, with occasional corduroy in the road; not a good place for your mom's car. At 1.6 (2.57) there is a short steep intermediate rated rocky climb. At 1.8 (2.90) there is a trail to the right with a gate across it; continue straight. At 1.9 (3.06) there is a second short steep rocky climb. At 2.1 (3.78) there is a sharp drop on the gravel road, and at 2.3 (3.70) another road goes off to the right. For the described ride, continue straight.

After this junction, the road goes back to an easy beginner rating. At 3.1 (4.99) there is a grassy track to the right; again continue straight. At 3.4 (5.47) a climb begins, the top of which is reached at 3.6 (5.79). After a fairly level section, the road drops moderately down to Highway 30, which is reached at 4.4 mi (7.08). The return is by the same route, on which you will have two nice drops to ride down.

Back at Perkins Clearing there are a couple of choices if you want to ride additional distance. One option is to ride north back toward Mason Lake. A second option is a little more complicated. On the ride map you can see the road which goes west from Perkins Clearing to the Sled Harbor trailhead. As part of the land swap, IP agreed to keep this road open for the

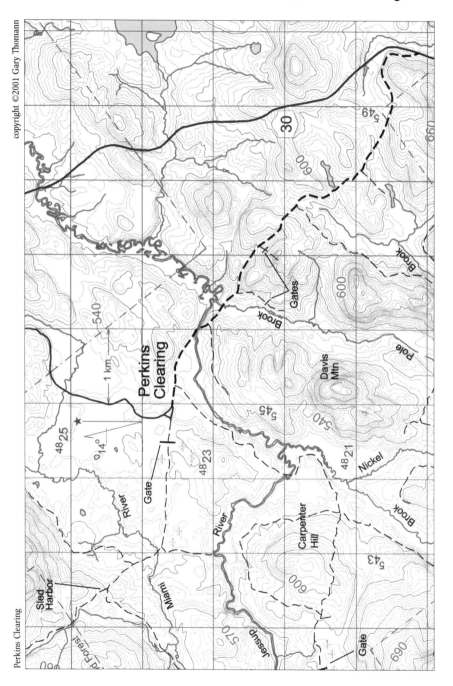

public. However, the signed agreement specified that the road was open only for hiking, skiing, snowshoeing, horseback riding and vehicles. Therefore, you can drive your car over to Sled Harbor but not, according to IP officials, legally ride your mountain bike. So, put your bike in the car and drive to Sled Harbor. From there you can ride northwest and enter Wild Forest classified public land. Unfortunately, you can ride only about one mile before you then encounter Wilderness classified land, in which of course you cannot ride. This small piece of Wild Forest land is the orphaned parcel that was mentioned earlier.

20

Sargent Ponds to Raquette Lake
Intermediate

Distance: 13.0 mi (20.9 km), can be lengthened

Difficulty: Easy intermediate

Climbing Required: 390 ft (120 m)

Time to ride: 3 to 4 hours

Wild Forest: Sargent Ponds

General

The picnic area on the Raquette Lake shore is a nice destination, via a trail you can ride with little mishap except for muddy feet and maybe a few scratches and insect bites. Much of the trail is singletrack, but unlike many narrow trails in the Adirondacks it is not completely filled with rocks and there are no big climbs or descents. In fact, except for a couple of marshy areas that have to be walked, the entire trail is rideable. The trail does have a lot of roots in it, and of course if it has rained recently and the surface is wet, the trail will be more difficult than described.

Trail Access

From the Village of Blue Mountain Lake go north 7.7 mi on NY 28N/30 and turn left (west) on North Point Road (there are signs for Buttermilk Falls and Forked Lake Public Campground). Or, go south 3.0 mi on 28N/30 from the Village of Long Lake and turn right. 6.3 mi after the turn there is a trailhead on the left, which here will be called the first trailhead. Continue to the second trailhead at 8.0 mi and park on the north side of the road (there is room for 2 or 3 cars). The trailhead elevation is 1790 ft (546 m) and the coordinates are 533930, 4858800.

Description

Start riding south on a dirt trail four to five ft wide, rated easy intermediate, with a few roots across the trail. You should see both hiking and orange snowmobile trail markers tacked to the trees. There will be some wet spots, just how wet will depend on the season and recent precipitation Be patient; the drier singletrack will begin later. At .33 mi (.53 km) there is a rideable log bridge. At .78 (1.26) you will drop down to cross a little stream.

Around 1.07 (1.72) Grass Pond appears on the left. The trail becomes a little narrower and tougher to ride. At 1.62 (2.61) there is a drop through a rock garden to a bridge across a small stream, rideable but tricky. The trail now becomes narrower. At 2.05 (3.30) you reach a T. On the return trip this will be a decision point. At the T, a sign states it is 1.7 mi to Upper Sargent Pond if the trail to the left is taken. To the right, it states that Tioga Point is 3.5 mi and Lower Sargent Pond is 0.1 mi. The actual distance to Tioga Point is about 4.4 (7.08).

Take the trail to the right and ride across a couple of small bridges. At 2.19 (3.53) you will come to a second T. You can pause here and look at the fish barrier if you want. Taking the trail to the left would get you to the Lower Pond leanto .38 mi (.61 km) away. For the ride as described here, again go to the right. You cross a bridge and then immediately face a short sharp climb that you may have to push up.

The wonderful singletrack begins here, with a one to two foot trail width, many small roots, and occasional bigger roots and rocks. There are also occasional short descents and climbs. At 2.53 (4.07) there is a trail to the left which goes down to Lower Pond; for this ride continue straight. At 3.42 (5.50) there is a split in the trail; take the left fork and walk through a wet grassy area. The trail will now begin to get a little more difficult, with more turns and roots. At 4.79 (7.70) there is a marshy area which is the inlet to Eldon Lake, which you will probably have to walk through. At 4.95 (7.96) there is a fork; an arrow points along the left fork; take it. At 5.25 (8.45) you are in a small valley and at 5.32 (8.56) there is an old trail to the left; continue straight. The trail now becomes easier again, and at 6.47 (10.41) you arrive at the end of Tioga Point overlooking the lake. There are numerous leantos and picnic areas at the

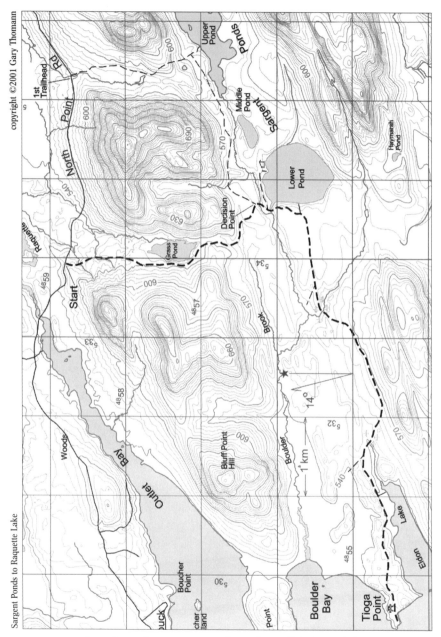

campground on the point, not to mention a beautiful view of the lake.

The return is by the same trail, and at the trail junction which was previously noted as a decision point you have a choice. A left turn to go north will take you immediately back to the cars on the trail you rode in on. If you want more of a challenge, go straight (east) on the trail to Upper Sargent Pond, a technically more difficult trail.

If you go east, ride for 2.0 mi (3.22 km) until you reach a T; the trail to the right goes to Upper Sargent Pond; the trail to the left back to North Point Road. Take the left turn (north). The trail remains singletrack, but immediately becomes much more difficult. It begins with a climb, followed by a couple of difficult climbs which you may have to walk. There are lots of rocks and roots in this advanced rated section. Then a descent starts and the first trailhead at North Point Road is reached after an exciting downhill section. The length of this section from the previous T is 1.1 (1.77). Turn left (west) on North Point Road and ride 1.7 (2.74) back to the cars.

There's nothing like making a splash.

21

McKeever - Bear Creek Loop

Intermediate

Distance: 13.4 mi (21.6 km) off road, 12 mi (13.6 km) of road riding

Difficulty: Intermediate

Climbing Required: 600 ft (180 m)

Time to ride: 3 to 5 hours

Wild Forest: Black River

General

A ride mostly on old roads, parts of which are rocky and eroded, with other parts having a soft surface with roots. It is 99.94% rideable for those with intermediate skills. There are a lot of other trails in this area, many of which cross the described ride. It is easy to do extra exploring if you want to increase the length of the ride or stay more than one day.

Trail Access

The ride begins near McKeever. From Highway 28, turn east onto McKeever Road 8.0 miles north of Woodgate (or the turn is just south of the Moose River about 11.0 mi south of the village of Old Forge). About 0.2 mi after turning, angle left and then back right between two old buildings and drop down onto a rocky road. Continue driving east on the rocky road to the trailhead, 0.8 mi after the turn off NY 28. The elevation at the trailhead is 1540 ft (470 m), its coordinates are 492670, 4828620.

If desired, a car shuttle can be used to eliminate the road riding. To do so, drive back 0.8 mi west to NY 28, go south 8.0 mi to Woodgate, and turn left (east) on Bear Creek road (at the blinking light). Go 3.2 mi east to the Bear Creek parking area and leave a car.

Description

There is a fork at the trailhead and two parallel roads go east. The left fork (northern road) is a beginner fire road. For the described ride take the right fork. This road is about 12 ft wide and probably muddy. Part of the time the surface is smooth and beginner rated, and then there are very rocky areas, including some tough rocky climbs in the first 0.6 mi (.97 km) which are intermediate rated.

At 1.3 (2.09) there is a crossing trail. The trail to the left (north) goes over to the fire road. The trail to the right goes south to Bear Lake. Continue straight. For the next kilometer or so, the road has fewer rocks, then regains its rocky character. There is a long rocky climb, with the top at 2.5 (4.02), followed by a nice rocky descent ending at a trail junction at 3.3 (5.31).

The trail to the left (north) crosses the jeep road and ends at Remsen Falls, which you can ride over to if you wish. For the mileage as listed here, take the trail going straight ahead, marked with a sign to Woodhull Leanto. The trail is an old dirt/mud road, easy intermediate until you reach 4.0 (6.44), and then becomes a little tougher. At about 3.9 (6.31) you may see a trail to the left; stay on the trail to the right. Then a junction appears at 4.8 (7.72), at the top of a climb.

Take the left turn and drop to the shore of Woodhull Lake at 5.0 (8.05). There is a small bench on the shore, and this is a good place to sit, rest, view the lake and have a snack. When ready to resume, ride back up the hill to the trail junction at 5.2 (8.37), turn left (south), go around the barricade and continue.

The trail becomes narrower and drops again. At 5.6 (9.01) there is a trail to the right that goes to Bear Lake. For this ride ignore it and continue south across a small stream that is the outflow from Bloodsucker Pond (nice name). Just past the stream there is a trail to the left which goes to a leanto on Woodhull Lake. For the described ride, again continue straight. At 6.2 (9.98) a small swamp appears, and there is about 100 ft of corduroy; probably the only section all day that has to be walked. For the next 0.4 (.64) the trail is wet and soft, with a lot of roots but few rocks. A snowmobile bridge over a creek is crossed at 6.6 (10.62). A wider old road is reach at 6.8 (10.94), take a right turn

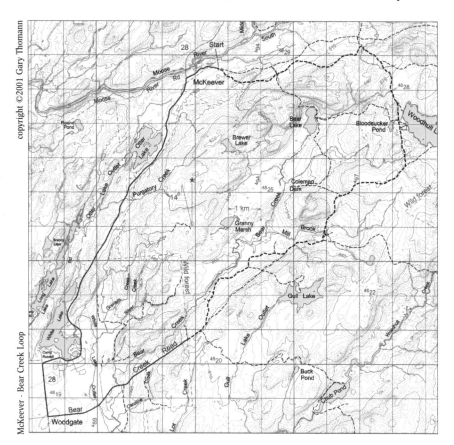

onto this road (the left turn should go down to Woodhull Lake).

The road is 12 to 15 ft wide with a soft dirt surface and an occasional rock. Technically, it is beginner rated; it begins to descend and you may find that you are riding very fast. Look ahead and keep control, whatever your speed. At 8.3 (13.35) there is a trail to the right to Coleman Dam. At this junction, there is a signboard with various mileages. The distance to the Bear Creek parking lot and the end of the off-road riding is given as 6.9 mi. This is inaccurate, the actual distance is about 5.1 mi. Continue straight ahead.

The descent on the road continues. At 9.2 (14.80) there is an unmarked singletrack trail to the right, followed by an unmarked snowmobile trail to the left. Continue straight. There is a small shack at 9.3 (14.96) with an old trail going back past it.. Again continue straight (southwest). There is a trail to the left at 9.4 (15.12) which goes east all the way to the falls at the outflow of Sand Lake. For the described ride, again continue straight.

At 10.2 (16.41) there is a fork, with a choice between two roughly parallel roads. Take the right fork onto an old road about 6 to 8 ft wide, which will be soft and perhaps muddy, rated easy intermediate. At 10.4 (16.73) there is a trail to the right, which appears to be abandoned; this may be an old trail to Coleman Dam. Continue straight. A trails comes in from the left at 11.2 (18.02); it probably crosses the parallel road and goes over to Gull Lake. As usual, continue straight.

The road widens to about 12 ft, with corduroy, rocks and wet spots, wonderful to ride. Trails come in from the right at 12.0 (19.31) and 12.2 (19.63); skip both and continue straight. The road now becomes easy riding, beginner rated. There is a junction with a wider road at 13.0 (20.92), which is the road parallel to the one you have been riding. Turn right onto this road and continue riding.

A trail to Chub Pond goes left at 13.1 (21.08). Continue straight ahead to the Bear Creek parking area, reached at 13.4 (21.56). If you have a car here, the ride is finished. If your car is at the starting trailhead, ride 3.2 (5.15) west on Bear Creek road to NY 28, turn right and ride north for 8.0 (12.87), then turn right on McKeever road and ride an additional 0.8 mi (1.29 km) to the trailhead.

22

Irving Pond - Peters Corners Loop

Expert

Distance: 11.7 mi (18.8 km) For loop and two side trips

Difficulty: Expert

Climbing Required: 1100 ft (335 m)

Time to ride: 3 to 5 hours

Wild Forest: Shaker Mountain

General

Holmes Lake is a scenic destination on a trail with lots of corduroy, which can be somewhat jarring, so strong riders with the ability to power over the corduroy will enjoy this ride most. As the corduroy would suggest, this trail is pretty wet. Still, the trail is completely rideable, save for some of the worst wet spots and a few short steep climbs.

Trail Access

Drive or ride east on Benson Road (112) from NY 10/29A just north of West Caroga Lake. At 1.5 mi Shutts Road goes off to the north. Turn left here and park alongside the road. The junction can also be reached from Upper Benson, by driving southwest down Benson Road (numbered 125 from that end) to Shutts Road. The starting point elevation is 1540 ft (470 m) and the coordinates are 544265, 4777320.

Description

Start riding north on Shutts Road, which is gravel. At 0.3 mi (.48 km) there is a house on the left, and the road surface changes to a muddy soft road. At 0.6 (.96) there is a snowmobile bridge across a little creek, and then a trail junction, with trails going to the right, straight ahead, and to the left. Take the trail to the left.

The old road continues soft, grassy, with rocks and the corduroy begins. These are logs about 6 inches in diameter which have been placed across the trail in the softest spots. They are bumpy but rideable. At about 1.0 (1.61) there is a fork in the trail; take the left fork, which has the trail markers on it.

After the fork is a climb with a lot of corduroy across the trail, and at 1.3 (2.09) the southeast edge of Irving Pond is reached. There are two signboards; one pointing forward on the trail (to Holmes Lake and Peters Corners) and the other points back to the start and Shutts Road. From this point there is also an old road going west along the southern edge of Irving Pond to a dam, and then on west to route 10/29A. However, for the described ride continue north on the soft trail with lots of corduroy, bumpy and demanding, but rideable. The trail crosses a little creek on a snowmobile bridge at 1.8 (2.90) and the corduroy continues. The south edge of Bellows Lake is reached at 2.3 (3.70), and the trail continues, 10 ft wide, soft and reinforced with the corduroy.

At 3.2 (5.15) a long rideable climb begins, the top of which is reached at 4.0 (6.44) at an elevation of 2050 ft (625 m). Then you begin to descend, but almost immediately, at 4.1 (6.60), there is a narrow trail going off to the left (north). Take this left turn, the described ride includes a side trip to Little Holmes Lake. This northbound trail is about 4 ft wide. At 4.5 (7.24) Little Holmes Lake appears on the right. It is possible to ride down to the shore. The trail continues on north, starts to drop and becomes a little more rocky, and at 4.7 (7.56) crosses a rocky stream, which is the outflow from Little Holmes Lake. The trail continues on north, but for the ride described here, turn around and ride back to the main trail, reached at 5.4 (8.69).

Back at the main trail, turn left and continue riding east. The trail descends, with the usual soft surface and a lot of corduroy, all rideable. At 5.8 (9.33) there is an old road going north to Holmes Lake, which you will also visit. Turn left and ride north.

The trail to the north will probably be muddy, and maybe even unrideable in spots. It is a climb to Holmes Lake, which is reached at 6.2 (9.98). Again turn

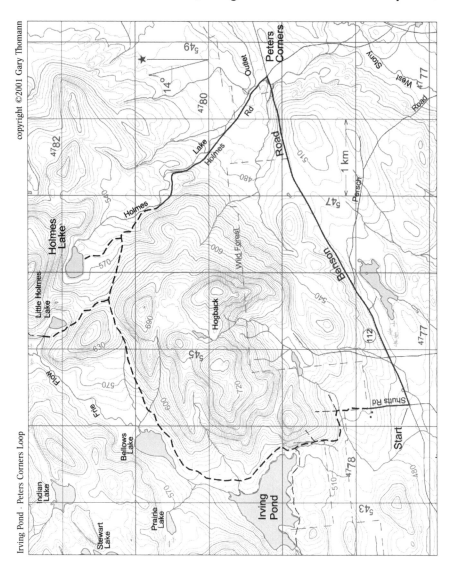

around and go back to the main trail, reached at 6.6 (10.62). The main trail turns south and descends, changing into a rocky and somewhat wet road. It is enjoyable riding. Benson Road (Highway 112) is reached at 8.6 (13.84) at Peters Corners. Turn west on the paved road and ride back to the start point, reached at 11.7 mi (18.83 km).

23
Stewart Landing - Caroga Lake Loop
Expert

Distance: 19.0 mi (30.6 km)

Difficulty: Expert

Climbing Required: 800 ft (245 m)

Time to ride: 4 to 6 hours

Wild Forest: Ferris Lake

General

This ride is a big rambunctious loop on snowmobile trails between Stewart Landing and the Village of Caroga Lake, almost completely rideable for expert riders. With a car left at the village of Caroga Lake, either the northern or southern part of loop could be ridden; the southern half has a firmer surface. All parts of the loop will probably be muddy in the spring, so this loop is best to ride during reasonably dry periods. Swimming is available at the finish. It is difficult to find a map that shows this trail, and my map may not show the exact trail position, since I have not taken GPS readings while riding it.

Trail Access

As described here, the ride begins from Stewart Landing. From NY 29 about twelve miles west of Johnstown take 119 north about nine miles to Stewart Landing Road. Turn right (east) and drive 3.5 mi to the end of the road and the dam. Park here. The elevation at the trailhead is 1535 ft (468 m) and the coordinates are 532995, 4776475.

To leave a car at Caroga Lake, drive back out Stewart Landing Road, turn right (northwest) on 119 and after a mile turn right (north) on Mallet Hill

Road. Go north about two miles to NY 29A, turn east for about eight miles, and then go south on NY 10/29A about six miles to the village.

Description

The loop is described counter-clockwise. From the dam at Stewart's Landing, ride back west about 100 yd on the road and turn left (south) on snowmobile trail #4. The trail drops to a bridge across Sprite Creek at 0.2 m (.32 km). There is an immediate test of fitness and power on a long intermediate rated climb on an 8 ft wide trail. The top is attained at 0.5 (.80).   There   is   an intersection at 0.7 (1.13). Continue on the trail more or less straight through the intersection, with orange markers and a sign to Glasgow/Crystal Lake. Later, you will hopefully come back to this intersection on the trail coming in from the left.

The trail goes through a series of short climbs and descents; continuing about 8 ft wide with an intermediate rocky sur-

We're supposed to ride this?

face. At 1.3 (2.09) there is an old trail going off to the left; stay to the right. Then the trail starts to drop, and at 1.6 (2.57) there is a fork. To the right is Crystal Lake (which I guess is another name for Tamarack Vly); take the left fork toward Glasgow Road.

The trail continues rocky and excellent for riding. At 2.5 (4.02) a small stream is crossed, followed immediately by a short steep climb. After the stream crossing, the trail becomes rockier and technically more difficult, expert rated. At 3.1 (4.99) there is a small building on the left. At 3.3 (5.31) there may be a large mud hole that has to be walked, then just after the mud there is a singletrack trail to the left; continue straight. At 3.5 (5.63) the trail crosses the Hillabrandt Vly outlet on a bridge that should be walked.

The trail continues upper intermediate to expert, and Hillabrandt Vly is seen on the left at 3.8 (6.11). Then there may be a series of wet spots, continuing to about 4.5 (7.24). There is a tough climb at 4.8 (7.72), and a long downhill begins at 5.0 (8.05). At 5.7 (9.17) there is a junction; for the described ride, turn right and ride a few hundred ft to the dam on Glasgow Lake. Apparently there used to be a clothespin factory here. This is a good place for a short rest and a snack. After your rest, return to the intersection, reached at 5.8 (9.33), and turn right (would have been straight from the original trail).

The long downhill continues, rocky and generally expert rated. It is exciting and enjoyable riding. The trail ends at 7.5 (12.07) when it careens into NY 10.

Turn left and start riding the highway toward Caroga Lake. At 8.0 (12.87) angle right onto Nick Stock road, which is gravel. This road rejoins the highway at 8.5 (13.68). At 10.8 (17.38), as NY 10 turns slightly to the right, angle off left on Caroga Lake Shore Road. This road rejoins the highway (now NY 10/29A) at 11.5 (18.50); turn left onto the highway. There are some small stores on the right, where you can reload with provisions.

Continue north on 10/29A to county highway 111 (Bridge Road) which angles to the left at 11.8 (18.99). Turn left on 111, and then immediately turn left again to head west on Morey Road, which is hard surfaced. When the hard surface ends at 12.4 (19.95), keep riding the old road straight (west) up a steep climb. The old road is about 15 to 20 ft wide, with a soft surface and some roots. The surface is not technically difficult, but the road continues to climb. A snowmobile bridge over a small stream is crossed at 13.4 (21.56); the bridge is slippery if wet. After the bridge, the trail becomes narrower, 5 to 6 ft wide, with rocks appearing in addition to the roots. The rating is expert, or nearly so.

The climbing eventually ends at about 14.6 (23.49), and the trail begins to descend. It remains rocky with roots, especially tricky if wet. The trail forks at 14.8 (23.81); take the left fork. There is another snowmobile bridge at 15.2 (24.46), and a grassy meadow is reached at 15.5 (24.94). Then there is a steep drop, and a bog is reached at 15.8 (25.42); it may be necessary to walk about 200 ft through this wet area.

The trail continues 5 to 6 ft wide with a soft surface filled with rocks and roots. The rating here is intermediate. Small bridges are crossed at 15.9 (25.58), 16.9 (27.19) and 17.1 (27.51). After the third bridge there is a sharp climb that is very difficult to ride successfully. To repay you for the climb, there is a long fast downhill, ending at a bog at 18.1 (29.12). Just past the bog at 18.3

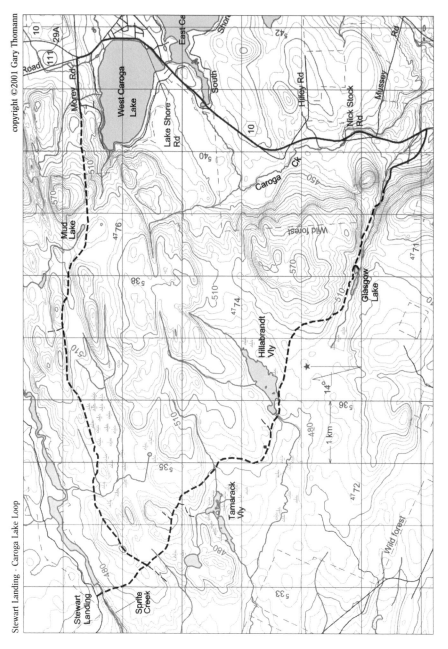

(29.44) there is a junction, which you were at before. Turn right and drop down to the bridge over Sprite Creek, climb back up to Stewart Landing Road and turn right to the cars, reached at 19.0 mi (30.57 km). After this marathon, if the weather is warm you will probably enjoy a dip in the lake.

northwest

The northwest area of the park has six small Wild Forests in it. Although the total area is small compared to the other three corners of the park, there still appears to be land enough for many trails. Unfortunately, this is the part of the park I am the least familiar with, partly because it is such a distance from the Capital District where I live. You are probably not interested in my excuses, but I have no other explanation for my poor knowledge of the northwest. I have managed to find and describe two enjoyable rides, both near the Cranberry Lake Campground.

24

Burntbridge Pond Trail
Intermediate

Distance: 13.8 mi (22.2 km) for round trip

Difficulty: Easy intermediate

Climbing Required: 700 ft (210 m)

Time to ride: 3 to 5 hours

Wild Forest: Cranberry Lake

General

This trail is partially on the old railroad grades of the Emporium Lumber Company, which sold the land to the state in 1933. The destination is the leanto at scenic Burntbridge Pond. It is a good trail for a beginner rider who would like to try an intermediate rated trail. There are a couple of short rocky intermediate rated sections and a small amount of singletrack, but the trail is generally 5 to 10 ft wide.

Trail Access

The trailhead is on the south side of Highway 3 east of the Village of Cranberry Lake. From the intersection of Highway 3 and Lone Pine road, which is the road from Highway 3 into the Cranberry Lake campground, drive 2.4 mi east on the highway. There is parking at the trailhead, with a signboard stating it is 6.5 mi to Burntbridge Pond (actual distance measured 6.9 mi by author). The elevation at the trailhead is 1475 ft (450 m), and the coordinates are 516750, 4898005.

Description

Start riding south on a grassy singletrack. The first .25 mi (.40 km) is narrow, but then the trail widens to 4 or 5 ft, beginner rated. The trail runs along a level corridor about 10 ft wide, which must be one of the railroad beds. At .3 (.48) ride across a snowmobile bridge, and then ride the half-dozen more that

Take the time to focus on the outdoors while taking a break from everyday life.

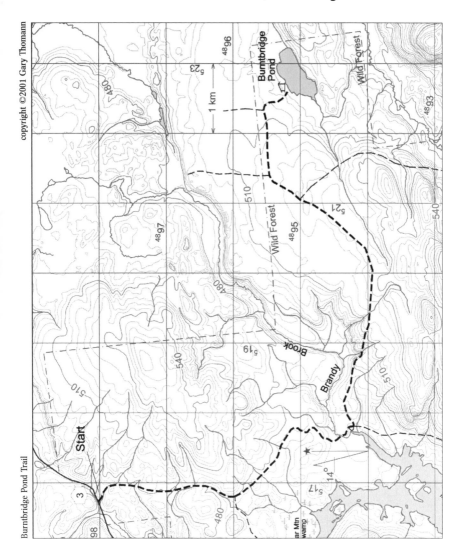

follow. They will be slippery if wet. At 1.1 (1.77) there is a short section of intermediate rated trail. At 1.5 (2.41) there is a junction. Continue straight ahead (south). The trail to the right (west) is the Cranberry Lake loop, discussed in the next description.

The grassy 5 ft wide trail continues, beginner rated. At about 2.3 (3.70) there may be some wet spots, and then the trail becomes rockier, rated easy intermediate. At 2.6 (4.18) a nice downhill begins, which ends at the bridge over Brandy Brook at 2.9 (4.67). At 3.0 (4.83) there is a side trail to the right; continue straight. At 3.1 (4.99) there is a four way junction. For the described ride, turn left (east). (The trail straight ahead goes to Curtis and Dog Ponds; and includes some expert rated singletrack).

After turning east, the trail gradually climbs for about 1.2 mi (1.93), although it may not be noticeable while riding. The trail widens to 8 or 10 ft with a leafy surface and a few rocks, still rated easy intermediate. You may notice the trees in this part of the ride are larger and older than those along the first south going section. At 4.1 (6.60) there is a rocky uphill stretch about 100 ft long, which is at least intermediate rated and difficult to ride in the uphill direction. Less experienced riders can walk it. At 4.3 (6.92) there is a rideable stream crossing. After the crossing there are more roots in the trail. At 5.6 (9.01) there is a trail to the right, which also goes to Curtis and Dog Ponds. The trail to the right may be overgrown. For the described ride continue straight.

At 6.0 (9.65) there is a fork. The left fork trail leaves the Wild Forest classified land in about 0.1 mi, at which point there is a sign with the words "Emporium Easement" on it. I do not know whether the easement land is open for riding or not. In any case, for this ride take the right fork and continue riding. At 6.6 (10.62) a trail comes in from the left, which is another trail into the easement lands; continue straight. There is a section of wet trail with corduroy at around 6.8 (10.94), and then the Burntbridge Pond leanto is reached at 6.9 (11.10), a nice place for a rest and a snack.

The return to the trailhead is by the same route. There will be a long gentle fun downhill approaching the four way junction, before you turn north toward the trailhead. It is possible to add a loop on the return by taking the Bear Mountain trail to Cranberry Lake campground. This trail is discussed in the next description.

25

Cranberry Lake Loop

Intermediate/Expert

Distance: 8.0 mi (12.9 km) for loop, 4.0 mi of this is on roads

Difficulty: Intermediate, with one expert section

Climbing Required: 400 ft (120 m)

Time to ride: 2 to 3 hours

Wild Forest: Cranberry Lake

General

This ride goes through the Cranberry Lake Campground. The off-road part is mostly rocky singletrack, rated intermediate, with a short section of expert rated singletrack. The first 1.5 mi uses the same trail as the ride to Burntbridge Pond. You can also begin this ride from within the Cranberry Lake campground.

Trail Access

The trailhead is on the south side of Highway 3 east of the Village of Cranberry Lake. From the intersection of Highway 3 and Lone Pine road, which is the road from Highway 3 into the Cranberry Lake campground, drive 2.4 mi east on the highway. There is parking at the trailhead, the elevation here is 1475 ft (450 m), and the coordinates are 516750, 4898005.

Description

Start riding south on a grassy singletrack. The first .25 mi (.40 km) is narrow, but then the trail widens to 4 or 5 ft, beginner rated. At .3 (.48) ride across a snowmobile bridge, and then ride the half-dozen more that follow. They will be slippery if wet. At 1.1 (1.77) there is a short section of intermediate rated trail. At 1.5 (2.41) there is a junction; turn right and ride west. (The straight ahead trail is the one to Burntbridge Pond in the previous description.)

The trail to the west starts off as singletrack and dropping, rated easy intermediate. It may have branches hanging into it. Ride across a bridge over a stream at 1.7 (2.74), and continue on rocky, intermediate rated singletrack, occasionally descending. A boggy area appears at 2.5 (4.02), spanned by two long (about 200 ft each) stringer bridges followed by a shorter one about 40 ft long. The stringer bridges are made from two parallel planks with a narrow gap between. They are rideable, but tricky. At 2.8 (4.51) there is a tough wet area that may not be rideable.

Next, begin climbing on intermediate rated rocky, rooty singletrack, reaching the top at 3.2 (5.15). After pausing to catch your breath, start descending a similar trail. At the bottom of a sharp drop, a trail junction is reached at 3.8 (6.11). The trail to the left (south) goes up Bear Mountain and then descends back into the Cranberry Lake campground. As you can see from the map, this trail is very steep; I have not tried to ride it. For the described ride, bypass the southern trail and continue straight (west).

The next 0.2 mi (.32 km) of trail is expert rated, filled with large rocks. Ride it if you want a tough challenge. A small parking lot inside the Cranberry Lake campground is reached at 4.0 (6.44). Turn right (north) onto the road and ride to Highway 3, reached at 5.6 (9.01). Turn right again and ride east on Highway 3 to the trailhead at 8.0 mi (12.87 km).

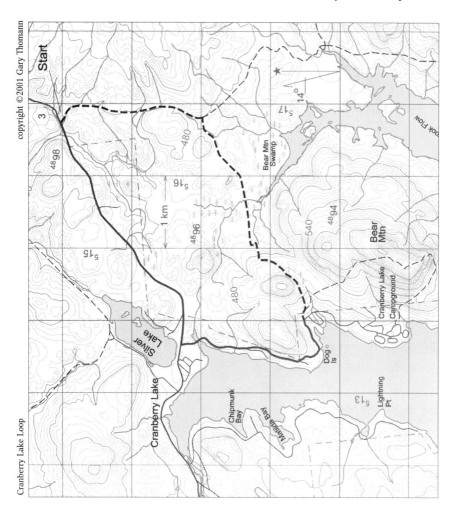

Cranberry Lake Loop

Additional Resources

Making studded tires

Studded mountain bike tires can be purchased from some tire manufacturers, but the studs are not long enough to reach through the snow cover and lock into the ice. As a result they do not work well for off road winter riding. Some bike shops will make studded tires using sheet metal screws, ask them to see. If not, they are pretty easy to make; here is the recipe.

Ingredients

2 mountain bike tires with large square tread blocks
2 old road bike tires, or other lining material
2 small mountain bike tubes
Two to three hundred phillips pan head 3/8 #6 or #8 sheet metal screws (or other similar pointed object)

Tools

Couple of electric drills (cordless work well)
Small finishing nail with the point sharpened
Phillips head bit
Pair of gloves

Directions

Buy sheet metal screws at a store that carries them in large boxes; if you buy them a dozen at a time in those little plastic sleeves you will have to mortgage the house. Put the finishing nail in one of the drills, and drill through each tread block, from the outside to inside. This will leave a small mark on the inside of the tire to show where to start the screw. Using the other drill and the phillips bit, carefully put the screw in from inside to outside, so the point of the screw comes out the center of the tread block. It may take some practice to get the screw to come out of the tread correctly. When fully screwed in, the point should stick out 3/16 to 1/4 inch. Less than this and the points won't reach through to the ice; more than this and you will pick up leaves and road kill. The 3/8 inch screws work with most tires. After all the screws are in, cut the old road tire and place it inside the mountain bike tire as a liner, so the tube will not touch the screw heads. The ends of the road tire will overlap an inch or two; just let them overlap. Put a little air in the mountain bike tube and put it in the tire; it should be cradled by the old road tire. Put on the gloves and mount the tires on your wheels. Especially when new, do not try to mount the tires with bare hands.

On ice, your bike will now go anywhere, uphill or down. In addition, the tires are so heavy that come spring you will have thighs the size of Alabama. Although you can go anywhere, don't ride where you are not allowed and don't bother animals. Maybe you'll be lucky enough to descend a snowmobile trail on which the fluorescent green ice surface softly glows in the pale February light.

A couple of additional tips. Pedals and cleats do not shed snow well and easily pack up. Carry a small screwdriver or something with a point on it to clean the snow out. Trail conditions usually vary, being combinations of those discussed above, and often trails will have unfrozen muddy sections. At the end of a ride, if your bike looks like a large frozen mud ball, do not take it home. Instead, go to a car wash and blast it with warm soapy water. The chain can be cleaned well holding the nozzle about an inch away with high pressure on. Then rinse the bike. At home put the bike in a warm dry place, and wipe it off with a rag. Oil the chain and moving derailleur parts with light oil. Wipe the rims and brake pads with a clean dry cloth; you want no oil on them. You're ready to go again.

Outdoor stores for maps, compass, etc.

The Mountaineer
Box 66, Route 73
Keene Valley, New York 12943
518-576-2281
www.mountaineer.com
*Hiking maps, compasses, books, Garmin
GPS*

Eastern Mountain Sports (EMS)
51 Main Street, Lake Placid, NY 12946
518-523-2505
www.emsonline.com
*Hiking maps, compasses, books, Garmin &
Magellan GPS*

High Peaks Cyclery
331 Main Street, Lake Placid NY 12946
518-523-3764
www.hpmac.com
Hiking maps, compasses, books

Jones Outfitters
37 Main St, Lake Placid NY 12946
518-523-3468
Some hiking maps and books

Nature Unlimited
59 Main St, Lake Placid NY 12946
518-523-8733
Some hiking maps and books

Blue Line Sport Shop
82 Main St., Saranac Lake NY
518-891-4680
Compasses, topo maps

Tip Top Sport Shop
40 Park Ave., Tupper Lake NY
518-359-9222
Compasses and some maps

Ames Department Store
Rt. 86, Saranac Lake NY
518-891-2850
Compasses

Ames Department Store
Rt. 3, Tupper Lake NY
518-359-3325
Compasses

Hickok's, 30
Fish Creek (Saranac Lake) NY
513-891-3328
Topo maps

Old Forge Hardware
Main St, Old Forge NY 13420
315-369-6100
Hiking maps, compasses, large book section

Old Forge Outfitters
Rt. 28, 4 miles south of Old Forge NY
315-369-6699
Hiking maps, compasses, books

Old Forge Department Store
Main St., Old Forge NY
315-369-6609
Hiking maps, compasses

Haderondah Company
Main St., Old Forge NY
315-369-3682
Hiking maps, compasses, books

Inlet Department Store
Main St., Inlet NY
315-357-3636
Compasses, some books

Moose River Trading Company
Rt. 28, Thendara
315-369-6091
Hiking maps, compasses, books
The Lake Store
Rt. 30, Indian Lake
518-648-5222
Hiking maps, compasses, books

Hoss's Country Corner
Lake St., Long Lake NY
518-624-2481
Hiking and topo maps, compasses, books

Beaver Brook Outfitters
Rts. 8 and 28, Wevertown NY
518-251-3394
www.beaverbrook.net
Hiking maps, compasses, books

Mountaineer Outdoor Supply
Route 28, Inlet NY
315-357-6672
& Route 28, Old Forge NY
315-369-6672
www.mountainmanoutdoors.com
Hiking maps, compasses, books

Bike Shops

High Peaks Cyclery
331 Main Street, Lake Placid NY 12946
518-523-3764
www.hpmac.com
Giant, K2, Specialized, rents bikes

**Mt Van Hovenberg Mountain Bike
Center (High Peaks Cyclery)**
Olympic Center, Lake Placid NY 12946
518-523-1655

Maui North Bike Shop
134 Main St, Lake Placid NY 12946
518-523-7245
Gary Fisher, Diamond Back, rents bikes

Placid Planet Bicycles
200 Saranac Ave, Lake Placid NY 12946
518-523-4128
www.placidplanetbicycles.com *Cannondale,
Kona, Litespeed, Schwinn, Trek, Kline,
rents bikes*

Mountain Run
359 Main Street, Lake Placid NY 12946
518-523-9443
www.boardertown.com/frames.html
*Iron Horse, Raleigh, Rocky Mountain,
Specialized*

Barkeater Bicycles
49 Main St, Saranac Lake NY
518-891-5207
GT, rents bikes

Pedals & Petals
176 N Route 28, BOX 390, Inlet NY
13360
315-357-3281
www.pedalsandpetals.com
Gary Fisher, Trek, rents bikes

The Mountain & Boardertown
Main Street, P.O. Box 44, North Creek
NY 12853
518-251-3111
www.boardertown.com/frames.html
*Trek, Rocky Mountain, K2, Foes, rents
bikes*

Large Park classification maps

*"Adirondack Park Land Use and
Development Plan Map,"*
NYS Adirondack Park Agency
PO Box 99, Ray Brook NY 12977 1999
518-891-4050
www.northnet.org/adirondackparkagency
*A 43 x 34" free map showing all land clas-
sifications, towns and main roads. Call
APA for a copy, or their headquarters is on
the north side of highway 86 between Lake
Placid and Saranac Lake.*

*"Adirondack Forest Preserve Map
and Guide"*
Published by DEC
call their Bureau of Public Lands:
518-457-7433
*A 35 x 27" free map showing public land
classifications, towns and main roads.*

"Adirondack Park"
The Adirondack Council
PO Box D-2, Elizabethtown NY 12932-
0640
518-873-2240
http://www.adirondackcouncil.org
$23
*A 42 x 36" color map showing public land
classifications, towns and main roads.*

"The Adirondack Park"
**Adirondack Maps Inc. (formerly Plinth,
Quoin and Cornice Assoc)**
PO Box 718, Market Street, Keene
Valley NY 12943
518-576-9861
http://www.adirondackmaps.com
*$4.95 + shipping
A 43 x 33" maps showing public land
classifications, towns and main roads.*

Car washes

Adirondack Car Wash
708 Quaker Rd., Queensbury NY 12804
518-761-0430 (not inside park)

Old Forge Car Wash
Main St, Old Forge NY
315-369-3435

Millcreek Car Wash
5407 Parkway, Lowville NY
315-376-2887 (not inside park)

Sunoco Inc.
Intersection Routes 73 & 86, Lake Placid
NY 12946
518-523-2672

Woodruff St., Saranac Lake NY

Book stores

Bookstore Plus
89 Main St, Lake Placid NY 12946
518-523-2950
also hiking maps

With Pipe and Book
91 Main St., Lake Placid NY 12946
518-523-9096
also hiking maps

Fact & Fiction Bookshop
17 Broadway, Saranac Lake NY
518-891-8067
also hiking maps

North Country Community College Book
20 Winona Ave, Saranac Lake NY
518-891-8494
also hiking maps

Keene Valley Bookstore
Route 73, Keene Valley NY
518-576-4736

Charlie Johns Store
The Four Corners, Speculator NY 12164
518-548-7451
www.charliejohns.com
also hiking maps

Adirondack Museum Shop
Rts. 30 and 28, Blue Mountain Lake NY
518-352-7311
also hiking maps

The Bookhouse
Stuyvesant Plaza, Western Avenue (Route
20) and Fuller Road, Albany NY, 12203
518-489-4761 www.bhny.com/index.html
*also hiking maps, not within park
boundary*

Adirondack ski areas with mountain biking

Gore Mountain
518-251-2411
http://GoreMountain.com/html/summer.htm
rents bikes

Whiteface Mountain
518-946-2223
http://orda.org/olypcsum.shtml#vanho
rents bikes

Mount Van Hoevenberg
518-523-3764
http://orda.org/olypcsum.shtml#vanho
*has mountain biking on their cross country
ski trails, rents bikes*

Garnet Hill Lodge & Cross Country Ski Center
13th Lake Rd, North River NY 12856
518-251-2444
www.garnet-hill.com
rents bikes

McCauley Mountain
Old Forge NY, 315-369-3225

Administrative agencies for the park

Adirondack Park Agency
P.O. Box 99, Ray Brook, NY 12977 518-891-4050
fax 518-891-3938,
www.northnet.org/adirondackparkagency/
Responsible for state and private land-use development plans within the Adirondacks Park to preserve and protect the natural resources.

New York State Department of Environmental Conservation (DEC)
50 Wolf Road, Albany NY 12223
518-457-3521
www.dec.state.ny.us/
Writes and enforces regulations for the Adirondack Park.

DEC Region 5 (Franklin, Clinton, Hamilton, Essex, Warren, Fulton, Saratoga and Washington counties)
PO Box 296, Route 86, Ray Brook NY 12977-0296
518-897-1200
www.dec.state.ny.us/website/reg5/index.html

DEC Region 6 (Herkimer, Jefferson, Lewis, Oneida and St. Lawrence counties)
317 Washington Street, Watertown NY 13601-3787
315-785-2239
www.dec.state.ny.us/website/reg6/index.html

New York State Office of Parks, Recreation and Historic Preservation
http://nysparks.state.ny.us

Non-profit/volunteer organizations involved with the park

Bike Adirondacks/Adirondack Park Mountain Bike Initiative
www.bikeadirondacks.org/

International Mountain Biking Association (IMBA)
PO Box 7578, Boulder CO 80306-7578
303-545-9011
www.imba.com.

The Adirondack Council
PO Box D-2, Elizabethtown NY 12932-0640
518-873-2240
www.adirondackcouncil.org/

The Adirondack Mountain Club (ADK)
814 Goggins Road, Lake George NY 12845
518-668-444
http://www.adk.org

Adirondack Forty Sixers
P.O. Box 9046, Schenectady, NY 12309-0046
www.adk46r.org/

The Association for the Protection of the Adirondacks
30 Roland Place, Schenectady NY 12304,
518-377-1452
www.global2000.net/protectadks

Hiking map sets

ADK Trail Maps
The Adirondack Mountain Club (ADK)
814 Goggins Road, Lake George NY 12845
518-668-4447
www.adk.org
$5.95 per map
These maps can be purchased at the club headquarters, by phone, online, and at most outdoor and book stores

"The Adirondack Series of Maps"
Adirondack Maps Inc. (formerly Plinth, Quoin and Cornice Assoc)
PO Box 718, Market Street, Keene Valley NY 12943
518-576-9861
www.adirondackmaps.com
$4.95 per map
Can be purchased at outdoor stores, and maybe by phone from the company

General park information on tourism, chambers of commerce, etc...

Adirondack Regional Chambers of Commerce
www.adirondackregion.org/

Adirondack Regional Tourism Council
PO Box 2149, Plattsburgh NY 12901
518-846-8016
www.adirondacks.org/home.html

New York Tourism
www.iloveny.state.ny.us/

The Adirondack North Country Association (ANCA)
183 Broadway, Saranac Lake NY 12983-1328
518-891-6200
www.adirondack.org/home.html

Hamilton County, New York County Office Building
Box 771, Indian Lake NY 12842-0771
518-648-5239
www.hamiltoncounty.com

Lewis County Chamber of Commerce
7383-C Utica Blvd., Lowville NY 13367
315-376-2213
www.adirondacks.org/lewiscounty

Fulton County Regional Chamber of Commerce & Industry
2 North Main Street, Gloversville NY 12078
518-725-0641 or 800-676-3858 www.fultoncountyny.org/

Old Forge, NY
www.oftimes.com/index.html

Saranac Lake Area Chamber of Commerce
30 Main Street , Saranac Lake NY 12983
800-347-1992 or 518-891-1990 www.saranaclake.com/

Tupper Lake Chamber of Commerce
60 Park Street, Tupper Lake NY 12986
518-359-3328
www.tupperlakeinfo.com/

Town of Long Lake Parks, Recreation & Tourism Department
PO Box 496, Long Lake NY 12847
www.longlake-ny.org/

The Adirondack Insiders Guide
www.insiders.com/adirondacks/

Glossary

Blowdown - Trees and brush that have fallen into and blocked a trail.

Corduroy - A mat of logs laid in a wet area of the trail. The direction of the logs is generally, but not always, perpendicular to the trail direction.

Doubletrack - A mountain bike trail wide enough that two bikes can pass.

GPS - The acronym for Global Positioning System. A set of orbiting satellites working with a receiver on the earth's surface. The receiver calculates position by measuring its distance to several of the satellites.

NAD27 - Called a datum, an approximate ellipsoid to model the earth, which is not quite spherical. This datum was developed in 1927.

NAD83 - A datum developed in 1983.

Singletrack - A narrow mountain bike trail that does not have room for two bikes to pass. The width is generally one to three feet.

UTM - Acronym for Universal Transverse Mercator. A method for putting the surface of the round earth onto flat paper.

Wild Forest - One of the classification types in the Adirondack Park. Mountain biking is generally allowed in Wild Forest classified land.